The Single Serving Entertaining Cookbook

pil

Publications International, Ltd.

Pictured on the front cover: Birthday Cake in a Jar *(page 128)*.

Pictured on the back cover *(top to bottom)*: Mac and Cheese Bites *(page 44)*, Individual Taco Salads *(page 84)* and Chocolate Chip Angel Food Cake Kabobs with Strawberry Sauce *(page 166)*.

ISBN: 978-1-63938-055-8

Manufactured in China.

8 7 6 5 4 3 2 1

Microwave Cooking: Microwave ovens vary in wattage. Use the cooking times as guidelines and check for doneness before adding more time.

Let's get social!
@ @Publications_International
@PublicationsInternational
www.pilbooks.com

Table of Contents

A New Way to Entertain

Even if you love entertaining, having a party can be a challenge. Hosting a party often involves putting out a spread with heaping platters of food where guests crowd around the table, share all the serving utensils and sometimes make a mess in the process. If you're looking for a calmer, neater and more orderly way to do this—perhaps due to health concerns, lack of space or too many children who aren't good at sharing—then the answer is simple: single servings.

Think Small

There are different ways to plan your single-serving menus. The simplest one is to cook dishes that already portion themselves out, such as mini quiches, chicken wings, sliders, wraps, empanadas, etc. Everyone loves finger foods; they work well for both kid and adult parties and for holiday get-togethers too. You can serve them on individual plates or small serving dishes—make the presentation as casual or as fancy as you like. You can also switch up your baking dishes, downsizing from large baking pans to muffin pans to create individual servings of traditional recipes such as Mini Spinach Frittatas (page 22), Mac and Cheese Bites (page 44) or Little Potato Gratins (page 70). Most of these recipes can be made in advance, removed from the pans and reheated when you're ready to serve.

Another individualized serving option is to use jars, which work especially well for salads like Greek Pasta Salad in a Jar (page 74) and desserts such as Brownie Ice Cream Treats (page 118). Like muffin pan recipes, jars can be prepared in advance, leaving you with more time to enjoy your party. And beyond their aesthetics—jar recipes are typically colorful and fun—jars are wonderfully portable, so they're perfect for outdoor celebrations and parties without formal seating arrangements, where guests take their food and find their own place to eat. Bring them to picnics, barbecues or get-togethers in the park to make your casual celebrations more special.

If you don't want to serve food in jars, you might try putting it on sticks. Skewers and sticks are available in a variety of sizes and materials and are wonderful tools for single servings—plus they're easy to prepare ahead of time. Main-dish kabobs are always a popular party food, pleasing both meat eaters and vegetarians alike. Choose from chicken, pork, beef, seafood, tofu or vegetable skewers that you can marinate before cooking or brush with sauce during or after cooking. (If you're using wooden skewers and grilling or broiling them, make sure to soak them in water for 20 minutes before cooking to prevent burning.) Then go beyond main dishes—you can skewer more foods than you might expect! Try melon balls and berries for brunch; cut-up veggies, cubes of cheese and/or cooked tortellini for appetizers or snacks; and chunks of cake, brownies or candies for dessert. Appetizer skewers can be paired with a spicy sauce, a vinaigrette drizzle or a ranch dip, while dessert skewers might be served with a drizzle of melted chocolate, caramel sauce or whipped cream.

Serve it Up!

If you love making big-batch meals for parties, you can still cook to your heart's content—you don't need to change the way you cook; just change the way you serve. You can make a big bowl of salad, a huge pot of soup or stew or a giant pan of lasagna, but instead of serving these dishes on a buffet, ladle or scoop out single portions onto individual plates, bowls or containers for your guests. Any toppings or condiments can be served in small ramekins or paper baking cups rather than communal bowls.

Contain Yourself

The key to single-serving entertaining is containers. Be creative! Snack mixes can be served in ramekins, paper baking cups or small bags, while individual portions of dip can be served in small glasses or plastic cups (stick the veggies or chips right in the dip). Sandwiches and wraps are already perfectly portioned, but they can be wrapped in butcher paper and tied with kitchen string, slipped into sandwich bags or served on plates or in paper boats. Single servings of soups, stews or chili can be served in small bowls or large ramekins, while other entrées like noodle dishes can go into Asian take-out containers. And jars make great containers for all types of salads, parfaits and desserts. You don't have to spend a lot on these items—you can find disposable containers of all shapes and sizes at dollar stores, warehouse clubs and party and restaurant supply stores. Or if you prefer reusable serving dishes, try shopping at thrift stores, dollar stores and craft stores which can be great sources for inexpensive plates, cups, glasses, bowls, jars, etc.

Single-serving entertaining is easy; sometimes it might just require a little more advance planning and a few extra supplies (depending on the number of guests you're having and the type of food you're serving). Whether you're hosting a birthday party, backyard barbecue or holiday open house, you'll find plenty of recipe ideas in these pages that are perfect for this new way to entertain.

Apple Cinnamon French Toast Cups
page 24

Brunch Bites

All your favorite brunch dishes—frittatas, hash browns, coffeecakes, even French toast—can be made in individual portions. And you can prepare them in advance, so there's no need for last-minute cooking. Just relax and enjoy your party!

Spinach Artichoke Egg Soufflés

Makes 8 servings

1 package (about 17 ounces) frozen puff pastry (2 sheets), thawed

1 teaspoon olive oil

¼ cup chopped onion

1 clove garlic, minced

¼ cup finely chopped roasted red pepper (1 pepper)

¼ cup finely chopped canned artichoke hearts (about 2 medium)

¼ cup frozen chopped spinach, thawed and squeezed dry

3 eggs, separated

4 ounces cream cheese, softened

½ teaspoon salt

⅛ teaspoon black pepper

4 tablespoons grated Romano cheese, divided

1. Preheat oven to 400°F. Spray eight 4-inch or 1-cup ramekins or jumbo (3½-inch) muffin cups with nonstick cooking spray. Unfold puff pastry; cut each sheet into quarters. Gently press each pastry square into bottoms and partially up sides of prepared ramekins. (Pastry should not reach tops of ramekins.) Place ramekins on baking sheet; refrigerate while preparing filling.

2. Heat oil in medium skillet over medium heat. Add onion; cook and stir 2 minutes or until softened and lightly browned. Add garlic; cook and stir 30 seconds. Add roasted pepper, artichokes and spinach; cook and stir 2 minutes or until liquid has evaporated.

3. Whisk egg yolks, cream cheese, salt and black pepper in medium bowl until well blended. Stir in vegetable mixture and 3 tablespoons Romano cheese.

4. Beat egg whites in large bowl with electric mixer at high speed 3 minutes or until stiff peaks form. Fold into vegetable mixture until blended. Divide mixture evenly among pastry-lined ramekins; sprinkle with remaining 1 tablespoon Romano cheese. Fold corners of pastry towards center.

5. Bake 25 minutes or until crust is golden brown and filling is puffed. Cool in ramekins 2 minutes; remove to wire rack. Serve warm.

Fruit and Waffle Parfait Cups

Makes 8 servings

2 cooked Belgian waffles, torn into bite-size pieces

1 cup raspberry jam

$3/4$ teaspoon almond extract

2 cups plain or vanilla yogurt

2 cups chopped fresh peaches or thawed frozen peaches

1. Divide waffle pieces evenly among eight parfait dishes.

2. Place jam in small microwavable bowl; microwave on HIGH 30 seconds to slightly melt. Stir in almond extract until smooth.

3. Spoon jam mixture over waffle pieces; top with yogurt and peaches.

Tip: You don't need parfait dishes to serve parfaits—you can use whatever you have in your kitchen. Try juice glasses, rocks glasses, beer glasses or wine glasses. You can also buy a set of inexpensive glasses for parties at dollar stores, or find them at thrift stores.

Mini Fruit Coffeecakes

Makes 12 servings

1 package (about 17 ounces) frozen puff pastry (2 sheets), thawed

1 package (8 ounces) cream cheese, softened

1 egg

2 tablespoons granulated sugar

1/4 cup desired fruit filling (apricot jam, strawberry jam, lemon curd or a combination)

1/2 cup powdered sugar (optional)

2 teaspoons milk (optional)

1. Preheat oven to 350°F. Spray 12 standard (2½-inch) muffin cups with nonstick cooking spray.

2. Unroll puff pastry on work surface; cut each sheet into six rectangles. Fit pastry into prepared muffin cups, pressing into bottoms and up sides of cups. (Two sides of each rectangle will extend up over top of muffin cups.)

3. Beat cream cheese in large bowl with electric mixer at medium-high speed until smooth. Add egg and granulated sugar; beat until well blended. Spoon heaping tablespoon cream cheese mixture into each cup; top with 1 teaspoon fruit filling. Snip center of each overhanging pastry with scissors or paring knife; fold resulting four flaps in over filling, overlapping slightly (as you would fold a box).

4. Bake 20 minutes or until pastry is golden brown and filling is set and puffed. Cool in pan 2 minutes; remove to wire rack to cool slightly.

5. Meanwhile, prepare glaze, if desired. Whisk powdered sugar and milk in small bowl until smooth. Drizzle over coffeecakes.

Upside Down Pancake Muffins

Makes 16 muffins (4 to 8 servings)

2 cups buttermilk pancake mix

1½ cups water

16 teaspoons maple syrup, plus additional for serving

1 cup fresh or frozen blueberries, raspberries, blackberries or a combination (do not thaw frozen berries)

Butter

Powdered sugar (optional)

1. Preheat oven to 350°F. Spray 16 standard (2½-inch) muffin cups with nonstick cooking spray.

2. Whisk pancake mix and water in 4-cup measuring cup with spout; let stand 3 minutes. Pour batter into prepared muffin cups, filling three-fourths full. Add 1 teaspoon syrup to each cup (do not stir); top with 1 tablespoon berries.

3. Bake 15 minutes or until tops are set and toothpick inserted into centers comes out clean. Loosen bottom and sides of cups with small spatula or knife; invert onto wire rack. If some berries stick to pan, gently scrape from pan and place on top of muffins.

4. Serve warm with butter and additional maple syrup. Sprinkle with powdered sugar, if desired.

Denver Scramble in Hash Brown Cups

Makes 12 cups (4 to 6 servings)

3 tablespoons butter, divided

1 package (20 ounces) refrigerated hash brown potatoes

1½ teaspoons salt, divided

6 eggs

2 tablespoons milk

⅛ teaspoon black pepper

⅛ teaspoon hot pepper sauce or to taste

½ cup diced onion (¼-inch pieces)

½ cup diced green bell pepper (¼-inch pieces)

½ cup diced ham (¼-inch pieces)

⅓ cup shredded Monterey Jack cheese

1. Preheat oven to 400°F. Spray 12 standard (2½-inch) muffin cups with nonstick cooking spray.

2. Melt 2 tablespoons butter. Combine melted butter, potatoes and 1 teaspoon salt in large bowl; stir to coat. Press potatoes into bottoms and up sides of prepared cups (about 5 to 6 tablespoons per cup).

3. Bake about 35 minutes or until bottoms and sides are golden brown. (Insides of cups will not brown.)

4. When hash brown cups have baked 15 minutes, whisk eggs, milk, remaining ½ teaspoon salt, black pepper and hot pepper sauce in medium bowl until well blended. Melt remaining 1 tablespoon butter in large skillet over medium-high heat. Add onion; cook and stir about 3 minutes or until softened. Add bell pepper and ham; cook and stir 5 minutes or until bell pepper is crisp-tender.

5. Pour egg mixture into skillet; cook 20 to 30 seconds without stirring or just until edges are beginning to set. Stir around edges and across bottom of skillet with heatproof spatula, forming large curds. Cook 3 to 4 minutes or until eggs are fluffy and barely set, stirring gently.

6. Remove hash brown cups from pan. Fill cups with scrambled egg mixture (about ¼ cup egg mixture per cup); sprinkle with cheese.

Berry-Quinoa Parfaits

Makes 6 servings

2/3 cup uncooked quinoa

2 cups plus 2 tablespoons milk, divided

1/8 teaspoon salt

1/4 cup sugar

1 egg

1 1/2 teaspoons vanilla

2 cups sliced fresh strawberries

1/4 cup vanilla yogurt

Ground cinnamon (optional)

1. Place quinoa in fine-mesh strainer; rinse well under cold water.

2. Combine quinoa, 2 cups milk and salt in medium saucepan; bring to a simmer over medium heat. Reduce heat to medium-low; cook, uncovered, 20 to 25 minutes or until quinoa is tender, stirring frequently.

3. Whisk remaining 2 tablespoons milk, sugar, egg and vanilla in medium bowl until well blended. Gradually whisk 1/2 cup hot quinoa mixture into egg mixture, then whisk mixture back into saucepan. Cook over medium heat 3 to 5 minutes or until thickened and bubbly, stirring constantly. Remove from heat; let cool 30 minutes.

4. Layer quinoa mixture and strawberries in six parfait dishes. Top with yogurt; sprinkle with cinnamon, if desired.

Asparagus Frittata Prosciutto Cups

Makes 12 cups (6 servings)

1 tablespoon olive oil

1 small red onion, finely chopped

1½ cups sliced asparagus (½-inch pieces)

1 clove garlic, minced

12 thin slices prosciutto

8 eggs

½ cup (2 ounces) grated white Cheddar cheese

¼ cup grated Parmesan cheese

2 tablespoons milk

⅛ teaspoon black pepper

1. Preheat oven to 375°F. Spray 12 standard (2½-inch) muffin cups with nonstick cooking spray.

2. Heat oil in large skillet over medium heat. Add onion; cook and stir 4 minutes or until softened. Add asparagus and garlic; cook and stir 8 minutes or until asparagus is crisp-tender. Set aside to cool slightly.

3. Line each prepared muffin cup with prosciutto slice. (Prosciutto should cover cup as much as possible, with edges extending above muffin cup.)

4. Whisk eggs, Cheddar, Parmesan, milk and pepper in large bowl until well blended. Stir in asparagus mixture until blended. Pour into prosciutto-lined cups, filling about three-fourths full.

5. Bake about 20 minutes or until frittatas are puffed and golden brown and edges are pulling away from pan. Cool in pan 10 minutes; remove to wire rack. Serve warm or at room temperature.

Breakfast Sausage Monkey Muffins

Makes 8 servings

8 ounces bulk pork sausage

1 egg, beaten

1 cup (4 ounces) shredded Mexican cheese blend, divided

1 package (12 ounces) refrigerated buttermilk biscuits (10 biscuits)

1. Preheat oven to 350°F. Spray 8 standard (2½-inch) muffin cups with nonstick cooking spray.

2. Cook and stir sausage in large skillet over medium-high heat 8 minutes or until no longer pink, breaking apart any large pieces. Spoon sausage and drippings into large bowl; let cool 2 minutes. Add egg; stir until blended.

3. Reserve 2 tablespoons cheese for tops of muffins; stir remaining cheese into sausage mixture.

4. Separate biscuits; cut each biscuit into 6 pieces with scissors. Roll biscuit pieces in sausage mixture to coat; place 7 to 8 biscuit pieces in each muffin cup. Sprinkle with reserved 2 tablespoons cheese.

5. Bake 22 minutes or until golden brown. Remove muffins to paper towel-lined plate. Serve warm.

Apple Cinnamon French Toast Cups

Makes 12 cups (4 to 6 servings)

1 loaf (16 ounces) challah, egg bread or brioche

1 cup milk

4 eggs

$\frac{1}{2}$ cup plus 2 tablespoons sugar, divided

$1\frac{1}{2}$ teaspoons ground cinnamon, divided

$\frac{1}{2}$ teaspoon salt

1 sweet tart apple, peeled and chopped ($\frac{1}{4}$-inch pieces)

Maple syrup

1. Preheat oven to 350°F. Spray 12 standard (2$\frac{1}{2}$-inch) muffin cups with nonstick cooking spray.

2. Cut bread into $\frac{1}{2}$-inch cubes; place in large bowl. Whisk milk, eggs, $\frac{1}{2}$ cup sugar, 1 teaspoon cinnamon and salt in medium bowl; pour over bread. Let stand 10 minutes or until most of egg mixture is absorbed. Stir in apple.

3. Divide bread mixture evenly among prepared muffin cups, filling to tops of cups.

4. Combine remaining 2 tablespoons sugar and $\frac{1}{2}$ teaspoon cinnamon in small bowl; sprinkle evenly over top of each cup.

5. Bake about 20 minutes or until apples are tender and tops are firm and lightly browned. Cool in pan 5 minutes. Loosen bottoms and sides with small spatula or knife; remove to wire rack. Serve warm with maple syrup.

Mac and
Cheese Bites
page 44

Individual Appetizers

Instead of dips and shared dishes, pass around platters of bite-size fun foods. Everyone loves classics like pizza, mac and cheese, burgers and guacamole—and now they can each have their own personal version of these tasty party favorites.

Tortilla Cups with Corn and Black Bean Salad

Makes 6 servings

3 tablespoons vegetable oil, divided

1 teaspoon salt, divided

1/2 teaspoon chili powder

6 (6-inch) flour tortillas

1 cup corn

1 cup chopped red bell pepper

1 cup canned black beans, rinsed and drained

1 small ripe avocado, diced

1/4 cup lime juice

1/4 cup chopped fresh cilantro

1 small jalapeño pepper, seeded and minced

1. Preheat oven to 350°F. Spray six standard (2 1/2-inch) muffin cups with nonstick cooking spray. Whisk 1 tablespoon oil, 1/2 teaspoon salt and chili powder in small bowl until well blended.

2. Stack tortillas; wrap loosely in waxed paper. Microwave on HIGH 10 to 15 seconds or just until softened. Brush one side of each tortilla lightly with oil mixture; press into prepared muffin cups, oiled side up.

3. Bake about 10 minutes or until edges are golden brown. Cool in pan 2 minutes; remove to wire rack to cool completely.

4. Combine corn, bell pepper, beans and avocado in large bowl. Whisk remaining 2 tablespoons oil, 1/2 teaspoon salt, lime juice, cilantro and jalapeño in small bowl until well blended. Add to corn mixture; toss gently to coat. Fill tortilla cups with salad. Serve immediately. (Tortilla cups and salad can be prepared ahead of time; fill cups just before serving.)

Tip: For slightly larger tortilla cups, use the back of the muffin pan instead. Spray the back of a standard (12-cup) muffin pan with nonstick cooking spray. Soften the tortillas and brush with the oil mixture as directed in step 2, then fit them between the cups on the back of the muffin pan. (Only about 3 will fit at one time, so two batches are required.) Bake at 350°F about 8 minutes or until the edges are golden brown.

Two-Bite Burgers

Makes 36 mini burgers

1 package (11 ounces) refrigerated breadstick dough (12 breadsticks)

1 pound ground beef

2 teaspoons hamburger seasoning mix*

9 slices Cheddar or American cheese, quartered (optional)

36 round dill pickle slices

Ketchup and mustard

*Or season with garlic powder, onion powder, chili powder, salt and black pepper.

1. Preheat oven to 375°F. Separate dough into 12 breadsticks; cut each breadstick into three equal pieces. Working with one piece at a time, tuck ends under to meet at center, pressing to seal and form very small bun about 1½ inches in diameter and ½ inch high.

2. Place buns seam sides down on ungreased baking sheet. Bake 11 to 14 minutes or until golden brown. Remove to wire racks.

3. Meanwhile, gently mix ground beef and hamburger seasoning in large bowl. Shape into 36 patties, using about 2 teaspoons beef mixture per patty.

4. Heat large skillet over medium heat. Cook patties in batches 7 to 8 minutes or until cooked through (160°F), turning once. Top with cheese slices, if desired.

5. Split buns in half crosswise. Place burgers on bottom halves of buns; top with pickles, ketchup, mustard and top halves of buns.

Spanikopita Cups

Makes 16 cups

6 tablespoons ($^3/_4$ stick) butter, melted

2 eggs

1 container (15 ounces) ricotta cheese

1 package (10 ounces) frozen chopped spinach, thawed and squeezed dry

1 package (4 ounces) crumbled feta cheese

$^3/_4$ teaspoon finely grated lemon peel

$^1/_2$ teaspoon salt

$^1/_4$ teaspoon black pepper

$^1/_8$ teaspoon ground nutmeg

8 sheets frozen phyllo dough, thawed

1. Preheat oven to 350°F. Grease 16 standard (2$^1/_2$-inch) muffin cups with some of the butter.

2. Whisk eggs in large bowl. Add ricotta, spinach, feta, lemon peel, salt, pepper and nutmeg; whisk until well blended.

3. Place one sheet of phyllo on work surface. Brush with some of the butter; top with second sheet. Repeat with two additional sheets of phyllo. Cut stack of phyllo into eight rectangles; fit rectangles into prepared muffin cups, pressing into bottoms and up sides of cups. Repeat with remaining four sheets of phyllo and butter. Fill phyllo cups evenly with spinach mixture.

4. Bake about 18 minutes or until phyllo is golden brown and filling is set. Cool in pans 2 minutes; remove to wire racks. Serve warm.

Quick and Easy Arancini

Makes 12 arancini

1 package (6 to 8 ounces) sun-dried tomato, mushroom or Milanese risotto mix, plus ingredients to prepare mix*

1/2 cup frozen peas or 1/4 cup finely chopped oil-packed sun-dried tomatoes (optional)

1/2 cup panko bread crumbs

1/4 cup finely shredded or grated Parmesan cheese

2 tablespoons minced fresh parsley

2 tablespoons butter, melted

4 ounces Swiss, Asiago or fontina cheese, cut into 12 cubes (about 1/2 inch)

*Or use 3 cups leftover risotto.

1. Prepare risotto according to package directions. Stir in peas, if desired. Let stand, uncovered, 20 minutes or until thickened and cool enough to handle.

2. Preheat oven to 375°F. Spray 12 standard (2 1/2-inch) muffin cups with nonstick cooking spray.

3. Combine panko, Parmesan, parsley and melted butter in medium bowl; mix well.

4. Shape level 1/4 cupfuls of risotto into balls around Swiss cheese cubes, covering completely. Roll in panko mixture to coat. Place in prepared muffin cups.

5. Bake 15 minutes or until arancini are golden brown and cheese cubes are melted. Cool in pan 5 minutes. Serve warm.

Sausage and Kale Deep-Dish Mini Pizzas

Makes 12 mini pizzas

1 tablespoon olive oil

4 ounces spicy turkey or pork Italian sausage

1/3 cup finely chopped red onion

2 1/2 cups packed chopped stemmed kale

1/4 teaspoon salt

1 loaf (16 ounces) frozen pizza dough or white bread dough, thawed according to package directions

3/4 cup (3 ounces) shredded Italian cheese blend

1/4 cup pizza sauce

1. Preheat oven to 400°F. Spray 12 standard (2 1/2-inch) muffin cups with nonstick cooking spray.

2. Heat oil in large skillet over medium-high heat. (If using pork sausage, oil is not needed.) Remove sausage from casings; crumble into skillet. Cook and stir about 5 minutes or until no longer pink. Remove to plate.

3. Add onion to skillet; cook and stir 4 minutes or until softened. Add kale; cook about 10 minutes or until tender, stirring occasionally. Return sausage to skillet with salt; stir until blended. Set aside to cool slightly.

4. Divide dough into 12 pieces. Stretch or roll each piece into 5-inch circle; press into prepared muffin cups. Sprinkle 1 teaspoon cheese into bottom of each cup; spread 1 teaspoon pizza sauce over cheese. Top evenly with kale mixture and remaining cheese.

5. Bake about 16 minutes or until golden brown. Cool in pan 1 minute; loosen sides with small spatula or knife. Remove to wire rack. Serve warm.

Cheesy Quichettes

Makes 12 quichettes

12 slices bacon, crisp-cooked and chopped

6 eggs

1/4 cup whole milk

1 1/2 cups thawed frozen shredded hash brown potatoes, squeezed dry

1/4 cup chopped fresh parsley

1/2 teaspoon salt

1 1/2 cups (6 ounces) shredded Mexican cheese blend with jalapeño peppers

1. Preheat oven to 400°F. Spray 12 standard (2 1/2-inch) muffin cups with nonstick cooking spray.

2. Divide bacon evenly among prepared muffin cups. Whisk eggs and milk in medium bowl until well blended.

3. Stir in potatoes, parsley and salt; mix well. Spoon evenly into prepared muffin cups.

4. Bake 15 minutes or until knife inserted into centers comes out almost clean. Sprinkle with cheese; let stand 3 minutes or until cheese is melted. (Egg mixture will continue to cook while standing.*) Gently run knife around edges and lift out with fork. Serve warm.

Standing also allows for easier removal of quichettes from pan.

Sausage Rolls

Makes 24 sausage rolls

1 pound ground pork

½ cup finely chopped onion

1 teaspoon coarse salt

2 teaspoons minced garlic

1 teaspoon dried thyme

1 teaspoon dried basil

½ teaspoon dried marjoram

½ teaspoon black pepper

1 package (17 ounces) frozen puff pastry (2 sheets), thawed

1 egg, beaten

1. Preheat oven to 400°F. Line two baking sheets with parchment paper.

2. Combine pork, onion, salt, garlic, thyme, basil, marjoram and pepper in medium bowl; mix well.

3. Working with one sheet at a time, place puff pastry on floured surface; cut lengthwise into three strips at seams. Roll each third into 10×4½-inch rectangle. Shape one sixth of pork mixture into 10-inch log; arrange log along top edge of one pastry rectangle. Brush bottom ½ inch of rectangle with egg. Roll pastry down around pork; press to seal. Cut each roll crosswise into four pieces; place seam side down on prepared baking sheet. Repeat with remaining puff pastry and pork mixture. Brush top of each roll with egg.

4. Bake about 25 minutes or until sausage is cooked through and pastry is golden brown and puffed. Remove to wire racks to cool 10 minutes. Serve warm.

Chicken Lettuce Wraps

Makes 6 to 8 servings

1 tablespoon
   vegetable oil

1 small onion,
   finely chopped

5 ounces cremini
   mushrooms, finely
   chopped (about
   2 cups)

1 pound ground
   chicken

¼ cup hoisin sauce

2 tablespoons
   soy sauce

1 tablespoon
   rice vinegar

1 tablespoon
   sriracha sauce

1 tablespoon
   oyster sauce

2 cloves garlic, minced

1 teaspoon grated
   fresh ginger

1 teaspoon dark
   sesame oil

½ cup finely chopped
   water chestnuts

2 green onions,
   thinly sliced

1 head butter lettuce

1. Heat vegetable oil in large skillet over medium-high heat. Add onion; cook and stir 2 minutes. Add mushrooms; cook 8 minutes or until lightly browned and liquid has evaporated, stirring occasionally.

2. Add chicken; cook 8 minutes or until no longer pink, stirring to break up meat.

3. Stir in hoisin sauce, soy sauce, vinegar, sriracha, oyster sauce, garlic, ginger and sesame oil; cook 4 minutes. Add water chestnuts; cook and stir 2 minutes or until heated through. Remove from heat; stir in green onions.

4. Separate lettuce leaves. Spoon about ¼ cup chicken mixture into each lettuce leaf. Serve immediately.

Mac and Cheese Bites

Makes 36 appetizers

3 tablespoons butter, divided

2 tablespoons all-purpose flour

1 cup milk

1 teaspoon salt

1/2 teaspoon black pepper

1 cup (4 ounces) shredded sharp Cheddar cheese

1 cup (4 ounces) shredded Muenster cheese

1/2 pound elbow macaroni, cooked and drained

1/3 cup panko or plain dry bread crumbs

Finely chopped fresh parsley (optional)

1. Preheat oven to 400°F. Melt 1 tablespoon butter in large saucepan over medium heat; grease 36 mini (1³/₄-inch) muffin cups with melted butter.

2. Melt remaining 2 tablespoons butter in same saucepan over medium heat. Whisk in flour; cook and stir 2 minutes. Add milk, salt and pepper; cook and stir 3 minutes or until thickened.

3. Remove from heat; stir in Cheddar and Muenster cheeses until melted. Fold in macaroni until blended. Divide mixture evenly among prepared muffin cups; sprinkle with panko.

4. Bake about 25 minutes or until golden brown. Cool in pans 10 minutes; remove carefully using sharp knife. Garnish with parsley.

Party
Popcorn
page 56

Single-Serving Snacks

Swap out big bowls of snack mixes, popcorn and nuts for smaller (and more creative) containers. Use ramekins, colorful paper baking cups, Asian take-out boxes, plastic cups or paper or plastic bags to provide your guests with individual portions of sweet and savory snack foods.

Choco-Peanut Butter Popcorn

Makes 6 servings

1/3 cup semisweet chocolate chips

3 tablespoons natural creamy peanut butter

1 tablespoon butter

4 cups air-popped popcorn

1/2 cup powdered sugar

1. Combine chocolate chips, peanut butter and butter in medium microwavable bowl; microwave on HIGH 30 seconds. Stir; microwave 30 seconds or until mixture is melted and smooth.

2. Pour mixture over popcorn in large bowl; stir until evenly coated. Transfer to 1-gallon resealable food storage bag.

3. Add powdered sugar to bag; seal bag and shake to coat. Spread on waxed paper to cool. Store leftovers in airtight container in refrigerator.

Ramen Border Mix

Makes about 6 cups

2 packages (3 ounces each) beef-flavored ramen noodles, coarsely chopped*

3 cups corn cereal squares

2 ounces cheese snack crackers

1 cup mixed nuts

3 tablespoons extra virgin olive oil

2 tablespoons prepared mustard

1 tablespoon Worcestershire sauce

2 teaspoons chili powder

1/8 teaspoon ground red pepper (optional)

*Discard 1 seasoning packet.

1. Preheat oven to 300°F.

2. Combine noodles, cereal, crackers and nuts in large bowl; mix well.

3. Whisk 1 ramen seasoning packet, oil, mustard, Worcestershire sauce, chili powder and red pepper, if desired, in small bowl until well blended. Drizzle over cereal mixture; toss gently to coat. Spread in single layer on baking sheet.

4. Bake 20 minutes or until mixture begins to brown, stirring after 10 minutes. Cool on baking sheet on wire rack 1 hour. Store in airtight container.

Citrus Candied Nuts

Makes 3 cups

1 egg white

1½ cups whole almonds

1½ cups pecan halves

1 cup powdered sugar

2 tablespoons
   lemon juice

2 teaspoons grated
   orange peel

1 teaspoon grated
   lemon peel

⅛ teaspoon
   ground nutmeg

1. Preheat oven to 300°F. Line baking sheet with parchment paper or foil.

2. Beat egg white in medium bowl with electric mixer at high speed until soft peaks form. Add almonds and pecans; stir until well coated. Add powdered sugar, lemon juice, orange peel, lemon peel and nutmeg; stir to coat. Spread nuts on prepared baking sheet.

3. Bake 30 minutes, stirring after 20 minutes. Turn off heat; let nuts stand in oven 15 minutes.

4. Transfer nuts from baking sheet to sheet of foil; cool completely. Store in airtight container.

Southwest Snack Mix

Makes about 6 cups

4 cups unsweetened corn cereal squares

2 cups pretzel twists

1/2 cup pumpkin or squash seeds

1 1/2 teaspoons chili powder

1 teaspoon minced fresh cilantro or parsley

1/2 teaspoon salt

1/2 teaspoon garlic powder

1/2 teaspoon onion powder

1 egg white

2 tablespoons olive oil

2 tablespoons lime juice

1. Preheat oven to 300°F. Spray baking sheet with nonstick cooking spray.

2. Combine cereal, pretzels and pumpkin seeds in large bowl. Combine chili powder, cilantro, salt, garlic powder and onion powder in small bowl; mix well.

3. Whisk egg white, oil and lime juice in separate small bowl until well blended. Pour over cereal mixture; toss to coat. Add seasoning mixture; stir gently to coat. Spread in single layer on prepared baking sheet.

4. Bake 45 minutes, stirring every 15 minutes. Cool completely on baking sheet on wire rack. Store in airtight container.

Party Popcorn

Makes 6 quarts

¼ cup vegetable oil

½ cup unpopped
   popcorn kernels

1 teaspoon fine sea
   salt or popcorn salt

4 ounces almond
   bark,* chopped

   Rainbow nonpareils

*Almond bark can be found
near the chocolate chips
in the baking aisle of the
grocery store.*

1. Line two baking sheets with parchment paper.

2. Heat oil in large saucepan over medium-high heat 1 minute. Add popcorn; cover with lid and cook 2 to 3 minutes or until popcorn slows to about 1 second between pops, shaking pan occasionally.

3. Spread popcorn on prepared baking sheets; immediately sprinkle with salt and toss gently.

4. Melt almond bark according to package directions. Drizzle over popcorn; sprinkle with nonpareils. Let stand until set.

Snack Attack Mix

Makes about 8 cups

4 cups unsweetened
   corn cereal squares
   or whole wheat
   cereal squares

1 cup pretzel sticks,
   broken in half

1 cup multigrain pita
   chips, broken into
   bite-size pieces

1 cup slivered almonds

2 tablespoons
   Worcestershire
   sauce

2 teaspoons canola oil

2 teaspoons paprika

1½ teaspoons
   cider vinegar

1 teaspoon salt

1 teaspoon garlic
   powder

1 teaspoon
   dry mustard

½ teaspoon
   ground cumin

¼ teaspoon ground
   red pepper

1. Preheat oven to 300°F. Combine cereal, pretzels, pita chips and almonds in large bowl; mix well.

2. Combine Worcestershire sauce, oil, paprika, vinegar, salt, garlic powder, mustard, cumin and red pepper in small bowl; mix well.

3. Drizzle Worcestershire mixture over cereal mixture; toss gently to coat. Spread in single layer on baking sheet.

4. Bake 10 to 15 minutes or until mixture begins to brown, stirring every 5 minutes. Cool on baking sheet on wire rack 2 hours. Store in airtight container.

Sweet and Spicy Beer Nuts

Makes 3 cups

2 cups pecan halves

2 teaspoons salt

2 teaspoons chili powder

2 teaspoons olive oil

½ teaspoon ground cumin

¼ teaspoon ground red pepper

½ cup sugar

½ cup beer

1. Preheat oven to 350°F. Line baking sheet with foil.

2. Combine pecans, salt, chili powder, oil, cumin and red pepper in small bowl; mix well. Spread nuts on prepared baking sheet.

3. Bake 10 minutes or until nuts are fragrant, stirring occasionally. Cool on baking sheet on wire rack.

4. Combine sugar and beer in small saucepan; heat over medium-high heat until mixture registers 250°F on candy thermometer. Remove from heat; carefully stir in nuts and any loose spices.

5. Spread sugared nuts on same baking sheet, separating clusters. Cool completely. Break up any large pieces before serving.

Parmesan Ranch Snack Mix

Makes about 8 cups

2 cups corn or rice cereal squares

2 cups bagel chips, broken into pieces

1½ cups pretzel twists

1 cup oyster crackers

1 cup shelled pistachio nuts

¼ cup grated Parmesan cheese

¼ cup (½ stick) butter

1 package (1 ounce) dry ranch salad dressing mix

½ teaspoon garlic powder

⅛ teaspoon ground red pepper

1. Preheat oven to 300°F. Combine cereal, bagel chips, pretzels, oyster crackers, pistachios and cheese in large bowl; mix well.

2. Melt butter in small saucepan over medium heat. Stir in ranch dressing mix, garlic powder and red pepper until well blended.

3. Drizzle ranch mixture over cereal mixture; toss gently to coat. Spread in single layer on baking sheet.

4. Bake 20 to 30 minutes or until mixture is lightly browned, stirring every 10 minutes. Cool completely on baking sheet on wire rack. Store in airtight container.

Miso Popcorn Crunch

Makes about 4 cups

4 cups air-popped popcorn

1 package (3 ounces) ramen noodles, any flavor, crumbled*

1 cup cashew nuts

2 tablespoons butter, melted

1 tablespoon miso paste

1 tablespoon water

Discard seasoning packet.

1. Preheat oven to 350°F. Line baking sheet with parchment paper. Combine popcorn, ramen noodles and cashews in large bowl; mix well.

2. Combine butter, miso paste and water in small bowl; mix well. Drizzle over popcorn mixture; toss gently to coat. Spread in single layer on prepared baking sheet.

3. Bake 10 minutes. Cool completely on baking sheet on wire rack.

Apricot-Pecan Snack Mix

Makes 4 cups

3 tablespoons butter

1 tablespoon lime juice

2 cups bite-size
   shredded wheat
   cereal

1 cup thinly sliced
   dried apricots

1 cup pecan halves

¼ cup packed
   brown sugar

1½ teaspoons
   chili powder

½ teaspoon salt

¼ teaspoon
   ground cumin

1. Preheat oven to 325°F. Line baking sheet with foil.

2. Melt butter in large saucepan over low heat. Stir in lime juice. Add cereal, apricots, pecans, brown sugar, chili powder, salt and cumin; cook and stir 3 minutes or until brown sugar is melted. Spread in single layer on prepared baking sheet.

3. Bake about 12 minutes or until cereal is toasted, stirring once. Cool completely on baking sheet on wire rack. Store in airtight container.

Individual
Taco Salad
page 84

Perfect Portions

Some dishes are just naturally easy to divide into single servings: Salads can be beautifully layered in jars, sandwiches and wraps are already in neat personal packages, and many side dishes can be made in muffin pans so everyone gets the right amount (with no passing or scooping required).

Little Potato Gratins

Makes 12 gratins (6 servings)

1 cup whipping cream

1 tablespoon fresh thyme

1 clove garlic, minced

1 teaspoon salt

$1/8$ teaspoon black pepper

2 pounds russet potatoes

$1/4$ cup grated Parmesan cheese

1 cup (4 ounces) grated Gruyère cheese

1. Preheat oven to 375°F. Spray 12 standard ($2^{1}/_{2}$-cup) muffin cups with nonstick cooking spray.

2. Pour cream into small microwavable bowl or glass measuring cup. Microwave on HIGH 1 minute or just until cream begins to bubble around edges. Stir in thyme, garlic, salt and pepper until blended; let stand while preparing potatoes.

3. Peel potatoes and cut crosswise into $1/8$-inch slices. Layer potato slices in prepared muffin cups, filling half full. Sprinkle with Parmesan; layer remaining potato slices over Parmesan. Pour cream mixture over potatoes; press potato stacks down firmly. Cover pan loosely with foil; place on baking sheet.

4. Bake 30 minutes. Remove pan from oven; sprinkle potatoes with Gruyère. Bake, uncovered, 30 minutes or until potatoes are tender and golden brown. (A paring knife inserted into potatoes should go in easily when potatoes are tender.) Let stand 5 minutes. Use small spatula or knife to loosen edges and bottoms of gratins; remove to plate. Serve warm.

Tip: Gratins can be made ahead, refrigerated and reheated for 10 to 15 minutes in a 350°F oven.

Grilled Cuban Party Sandwich

Makes 6 servings

¾ cup plus
  1 tablespoon
  olive oil, divided

6 tablespoons
  lime juice

4 cloves garlic, minced

2¼ teaspoons salt

¾ teaspoon black
  pepper

2 boneless skinless
  chicken breasts
  (about 8 ounces
  total)

1 medium yellow onion

1 loaf ciabatta bread
  (16 ounces), cut in
  half horizontally

¼ cup chopped
  fresh cilantro

6 ounces fresh
  mozzarella, sliced

1 medium tomato,
  thinly sliced

1. Whisk ¾ cup oil, lime juice, garlic, 2¼ teaspoons salt and ¾ teaspoon pepper in medium bowl until well blended. Pour ¼ cup marinade into shallow dish or quart-size resealable food storage bag. Add chicken; turn to coat. Cover and refrigerate up to 2 hours. Reserve remaining marinade.

2. Oil grid. Prepare grill for direct cooking. Cut onion crosswise into ½-inch-thick slices, leaving rings intact. Thread onion onto skewers.

3. Remove chicken from marinade; discard marinade. Grill chicken, uncovered, about 6 minutes per side or until no longer pink in center. Brush onion slices with remaining 1 tablespoon oil; place on grill next to chicken. Grill onion 4 to 6 minutes per side or until soft and browned.

4. Transfer chicken and onion to cutting board. Let chicken stand 10 minutes before slicing thinly. Season onion with salt and pepper; remove from skewers and separate rings. Toast cut sides of bread on grill.

5. To assemble sandwich, stir reserved marinade; brush on both cut sides of bread. Sprinkle cilantro over bottom half of bread; top with cheese, tomato, chicken, onion and top half of bread. Press down firmly; wrap sandwich tightly in foil.

6. Place sandwich on grill; top with large, heavy skillet to flatten.* Grill sandwich 4 to 6 minutes or until cheese melts. Cut into six pieces. Serve immediately.

Or use a brick wrapped in clean foil to weigh down sandwich.

Greek Pasta Salad in a Jar

Makes 6 (1-pint) servings

Pasta Salad

- 6 cups cooked rotini pasta
- 1½ cups diced cucumber
- 1 cup diced tomatoes (about 2 medium)
- 1 cup diced green bell pepper (about 1 medium)
- 1 package (4 ounces) crumbled feta cheese
- 12 medium pitted black olives, sliced
- ¼ cup chopped fresh dill

Dressing

- ¼ cup olive oil
- ¼ cup lemon juice
- ¼ teaspoon salt
- ¼ teaspoon dried oregano
- ⅛ teaspoon black pepper

1. For salad, combine pasta, cucumber, tomatoes, bell pepper, cheese, olives and dill in large bowl.

2. For dressing, whisk oil, lemon juice, salt, oregano and black pepper in small bowl until well blended. Pour over pasta; toss well to coat.

3. Spoon about 2 cups pasta salad into each of six 1-pint jars. Seal jars; refrigerate until ready to serve.

Mu Shu Pork Wraps

Makes 4 servings

1 tablespoon dark
   sesame oil

1 red bell pepper,
   cut into short,
   thin strips

1 small pork tenderloin
   (about 12 ounces),
   cut into strips

1 medium zucchini or
   summer squash or
   a combination,
   cut into strips

3 cloves garlic, minced

2 cups prepared
   coleslaw mix or
   shredded cabbage

2 tablespoons
   hoisin sauce

4 (10-inch) wraps

$\frac{1}{4}$ cup plum sauce

1. Heat oil in large nonstick skillet over medium-high heat. Add bell pepper; cook and stir 2 minutes. Add pork, zucchini and garlic; cook and stir 4 to 5 minutes or until pork is cooked through and vegetables are crisp-tender.

2. Add coleslaw mix to skillet; cook and stir 2 minutes or until wilted. Add hoisin sauce; cook and stir 1 minute.

3. Heat wraps according to package directions. Spread plum sauce down centers of wraps; top with pork mixture. Roll up tightly; cut wraps diagonally in half.

Mini Cherry Kugel

Makes 12 kugels (4 to 6 servings)

4 ounces uncooked egg noodles, broken into small pieces (1½ cups)

1 teaspoon salt, divided

4 eggs

1 cup ricotta cheese

½ cup sour cream

½ cup whipping cream

3 tablespoons sugar

½ cup dried sweetened cherries, chopped

1. Preheat oven to 350°F. Spray 12 mini (1¾-inch) muffin cups with nonstick cooking spray.

2. Cook noodles with ½ teaspoon salt according to package directions; drain well.

3. Beat eggs, ricotta, sour cream, cream, sugar and remaining ½ teaspoon salt in large bowl with electric mixer at medium speed until blended. Stir in noodles and cherries. Spoon into prepared muffin cups, filling three-fourths full.

4. Bake 50 minutes or until puffed and golden. Cool in pan 1 minute; remove to serving platter.

Caesar Salad in Parmesan Cups

Makes 6 servings

1³/₄ cups shredded Parmesan cheese, divided

1 small head romaine lettuce (10 to 12 ounces)

Salt

1 teaspoon Dijon mustard

1 teaspoon anchovy paste *or* 2 anchovy fillets, minced

1 clove garlic, minced

¹/₄ teaspoon black pepper

¹/₄ cup lemon juice

¹/₃ cup grated Parmesan cheese*

¹/₃ cup extra virgin olive oil

¹/₂ cup croutons

Parmesan used in the dressing should be finely grated to blend properly. Larger shreds of Parmesan work best for the cups.

1. Preheat oven to 375°F. Line baking sheet with silicone baking mat or parchment paper. Set standard 12-cup muffin pan upside down on work surface.

2. Place ¹/₄ cup shredded Parmesan in mound on prepared baking sheet; spread into 5-inch circle. Repeat to form six circles total, spacing circles at least 1 inch apart.

3. Bake about 8 minutes or until cheese is golden brown and bubbly. Immediately remove from baking sheet with thin metal spatula; place cheese rounds over back of upside-down muffin cups. Press down firmly to mold cheese rounds into cups. Cool completely on muffin pan to set bowl shape.

4. Meanwhile, prepare salad. Cut romaine leaves crosswise into 1-inch pieces. (Cut large leaves in half lengthwise before cutting crosswise.) Place in large bowl; sprinkle with salt. Whisk mustard, anchovy paste, garlic and pepper in medium bowl. Add lemon juice and grated Parmesan; whisk until blended. Gradually whisk in oil until well blended. Add half of dressing to romaine; toss to coat. Add additional dressing if necessary; reserve remaining dressing for another use.

5. Fill Parmesan cups with salad (about 1 cup salad per cup); top with croutons and remaining ¹/₄ cup shredded Parmesan.

New Orleans-Style Muffaletta

Makes 4 to 6 servings

¾ cup pitted
   green olives

½ cup pitted
   kalamata olives

½ cup giardiniera
   (Italian-style
   pickled vegetables),
   drained

2 tablespoons fresh
   parsley leaves

2 tablespoons capers

1 clove garlic, minced

2 tablespoons olive oil

1 tablespoon red
   wine vinegar

1 (8-inch) round
   Italian loaf
   (16 to 22 ounces)

8 ounces thinly sliced
   ham

8 ounces thinly sliced
   Genoa salami

6 ounces thinly sliced
   provolone cheese

1. Combine olives, giardiniera, parsley, capers and garlic in food processor; pulse until coarsely chopped and no large pieces remain. Transfer to small bowl; stir in oil and vinegar until well blended. Cover and refrigerate several hours or overnight to blend flavors.

2. Cut bread in half crosswise. Spread two thirds of olive salad over bottom half of bread; layer with ham, salami and cheese. Spread remaining olive salad over cheese; top with top half of bread, pressing down slightly to compress. Wrap sandwich with plastic wrap; let stand 1 hour to blend flavors.

3. To serve sandwich warm, preheat oven to 350°F. Remove plastic wrap; wrap sandwich loosely in foil. Bake 5 to 10 minutes or just until sandwich is slightly warm and cheese begins to melt. Cut into wedges.

Individual Taco Salads

Makes 4 (1-quart) servings

Dressing

1/4 cup mayonnaise

1/4 cup plain yogurt
or sour cream

1 tablespoon lime juice

1/2 teaspoon chipotle
chili powder

1 clove garlic, minced

1/4 cup crumbled
cotija cheese

1/4 cup chopped
fresh cilantro

Salad

1 tablespoon
vegetable oil

1 package (16 ounces)
frozen corn

1/4 teaspoon salt

1 large avocado, diced

1 teaspoon lime juice

1 can (about
15 ounces) black
beans, rinsed
and drained

2 medium tomatoes,
seeded and diced
(1 cup)

1/2 cup finely chopped
red onion

Packaged tortilla
strips or chips

Chopped romaine
lettuce

1. For dressing, whisk mayonnaise, yogurt, 1 tablespoon lime juice, chili powder and garlic in small bowl until well blended. Stir in cheese and cilantro.

2. For salad, heat oil in medium saucepan over high heat. Add corn; cook 10 to 15 minutes or until lightly browned, stirring occasionally. Stir in salt. Transfer to medium bowl; cool to room temperature. Combine avocado and 1 teaspoon lime juice in small bowl; toss to coat.

3. Pour 2 1/2 tablespoons dressing into each of four 1-quart jars. Top with 1/2 cup corn, scant 1/2 cup black beans, 1/4 cup tomatoes, 2 tablespoons red onion, 1/4 cup avocado, tortilla strips and lettuce.

4. Seal jars; refrigerate until ready to serve.

Note: Taco salads can also be made without the lettuce; use four 1-pint jars instead of the larger quart size.

Cacio e Pepe Cups

Makes 12 cups (4 to 6 servings)

8 ounces uncooked spaghetti, broken in half

2 eggs

1/4 teaspoon coarsely ground black pepper, plus additional for garnish

3/4 cup finely shredded or grated Parmesan cheese, divided

Minced fresh parsley

1. Preheat oven to 350°F. Spray 12 standard (2½-inch) muffin cups with nonstick cooking spray.

2. Cook pasta in large saucepan of boiling salted water until al dente. Drain pasta, reserving about 1 tablespoon cooking water.

3. Meanwhile, beat eggs and 1/4 teaspoon pepper in medium bowl. Stir in 1/2 cup cheese. Add hot pasta and reserved cooking water; stir until well blended and cheese is melted.

4. Divide spaghetti among prepared muffin cups (tongs work best); pour any remaining egg mixture from bowl into cups. Sprinkle tops with remaining 1/4 cup cheese and additional pepper.

5. Bake 15 minutes or until tops are set, no longer shiny and lightly browned. Immediately remove from pan. Sprinkle with parsley; serve warm.

Chicken, Hummus and Vegetable Wraps

Makes 4 servings

3/4 cup hummus (regular, roasted red pepper or roasted garlic)

4 (8- to 10-inch) sun-dried tomato or spinach wraps or whole wheat tortillas

2 cups chopped cooked chicken breast

Hot pepper sauce (optional)

1/2 cup shredded carrots

1/2 cup chopped unpeeled cucumber

1/2 cup thinly sliced radishes

2 tablespoons chopped fresh mint or basil

1. Spread hummus evenly over wraps. Arrange chicken over hummus; sprinkle with hot pepper sauce, if desired. Top with carrots, cucumber, radishes and mint.

2. Roll up tightly to enclose filling. Cut wraps in half diagonally.

Italian Bread Salad in a Jar

Makes 4 (1-pint) servings

4 slices Italian bread, cut into $\frac{1}{2}$-inch cubes (about 4 cups)

$\frac{1}{2}$ cup buttermilk

1 clove garlic, minced

1 tablespoon minced fresh dill *or* 1 teaspoon dried dill weed

$1\frac{1}{2}$ teaspoons onion powder

$\frac{1}{4}$ teaspoon salt, plus additional to taste

$\frac{1}{4}$ teaspoon black pepper

$\frac{1}{2}$ cup cherry tomatoes, quartered

1 cucumber, peeled, cut in half lengthwise, seeded and thinly sliced

1 stalk celery, thinly sliced

2 tablespoons minced fresh basil

1. Preheat oven to 400°F. Spread bread cubes on baking sheet. Bake 5 to 7 minutes or until lightly toasted and dry, stirring occasionally. Remove to medium bowl to cool.

2. Whisk buttermilk, garlic, dill, onion powder, $\frac{1}{4}$ teaspoon salt and pepper in small bowl until well blended. Let stand 15 minutes to allow flavors to blend.

3. Divide bread cubes evenly among four 1-pint jars. Layer tomatoes, cucumber, celery and basil over bread. Sprinkle with additional salt, if desired.

4. Stir dressing; pour equal amounts over salads. Seal jars; shake to distribute dressing. Refrigerate until ready to serve.

Marinated
Beef
Brochettes
page 104

Savory Skewers

Not only are skewers perfect for individual servings, but they're also a convenient party food because they can be assembled in advance. Choose from a wide variety of chicken, beef, seafood and vegetarian options—there's a kabob for every taste and every type of celebration.

Mediterranean Chicken Kabobs

Makes 8 servings

2 pounds boneless skinless chicken breasts or chicken tenders, cut into 1-inch pieces

1 small eggplant, peeled and cut into 1-inch pieces

1 medium zucchini, cut crosswise into 1/2-inch slices

4 medium onions, each cut into 8 wedges

16 medium mushrooms, stemmed

32 cherry tomatoes

1 cup chicken broth

2/3 cup balsamic vinegar

3 tablespoons olive oil

2 tablespoons dried mint

4 teaspoons dried basil

1 tablespoon dried oregano

1 teaspoon salt

Hot cooked couscous (optional)

1. Alternately thread chicken, eggplant, zucchini, onions, mushrooms and tomatoes onto 16 metal skewers; place in large glass baking dish.

2. Combine broth, vinegar, oil, mint, basil, oregano and salt in small bowl; mix well. Pour over kabobs in baking dish; cover and marinate in refrigerator 2 hours, turning occasionally.

3. Preheat broiler. Line broiler pan or baking sheet with foil.

4. Remove kabobs from marinade; discard marinade. Place kabobs on prepared broiler pan.

5. Broil kabobs 6 inches from heat 5 to 7 minutes per side or until chicken is cooked through. Serve with couscous, if desired.

Beef Spiedini

Makes 4 servings

1/4 cup olive oil

1/4 cup dry red wine

2 cloves garlic, minced

1 teaspoon
   dried rosemary

1 teaspoon salt,
   divided

1/2 teaspoon
   dried thyme

1/2 teaspoon coarsely
   ground black
   pepper

1 1/2 pounds beef top
   sirloin steak, cut
   into 1×1 1/4-inch
   pieces

6 cups water

1 cup uncooked orzo

1 tablespoon butter

1 tablespoon chopped
   fresh parsley

   Fresh rosemary
   sprigs (optional)

1. Combine oil, wine, garlic, dried rosemary, 1/2 teaspoon salt, thyme and pepper in small bowl; mix well. Place beef in large resealable food storage bag. Pour wine mixture over beef; seal bag and turn to coat. Marinate in refrigerator 15 to 30 minutes.

2. Oil grid. Prepare grill for direct cooking. Soak eight 6- to 8-inch wooden skewers in water 20 minutes.

3. Combine 6 cups water and remaining 1/2 teaspoon salt in medium saucepan; bring to a boil over high heat. Add orzo; reduce heat to low and cook 15 minutes or until tender. Drain orzo; return to saucepan. Stir in butter and parsley; keep warm.

4. Thread beef onto skewers.

5. Grill skewers over medium-high heat 8 to 10 minutes, turning occasionally. Serve with orzo. Garnish with fresh rosemary.

Tip: Rosemary skewers and brushes infuse the wonderful scent of rosemary into grilled foods. To make rosemary skewers, find large heavy sprigs and remove the leaves from the bottom three-quarters of the sprigs. Then thread small pieces of meat on each sprig before grilling. Or, to make an aromatic brush, bundle sprigs of rosemary together, tie with kitchen string and use as a brush for spreading sauces.

Jamaican Shrimp and Pineapple Kabobs

Makes 8 servings

1 cup prepared
jerk sauce

1/2 cup pineapple
preserves

1/4 cup minced
fresh chives

2 pounds large raw
shrimp, peeled
and deveined
(with tails on)

1 medium pineapple,
peeled, cored and
cut into 1-inch
cubes

4 large red, green or
yellow bell peppers
(or a combination),
cut into 1-inch
pieces

1. Oil grid. Prepare grill for direct cooking. Soak eight wooden skewers in water 20 minutes.

2. Combine jerk sauce, preserves and chives in small bowl; mix well. Reserve 1 cup sauce mixture for serving.

3. Alternately thread shrimp, pineapple and bell peppers onto skewers; brush with remaining jerk sauce mixture.

4. Grill kabobs over over medium-hot heat 3 to 5 minutes per side or until shrimp are pink and opaque. Serve with reserved jerk sauce mixture.

Serving Suggestion: Serve with hot cooked rice or orzo.

Barbecue Seitan Skewers

Makes 4 servings

1 package (8 ounces)
   seitan, cubed

½ cup barbecue sauce,
   divided

1 red bell pepper,
   cut into 12 pieces

1 green bell pepper,
   cut into 12 pieces

12 cremini mushrooms

1 zucchini, cut into
   12 pieces

1. Place seitan in medium bowl. Add ¼ cup barbecue sauce; stir to coat. Marinate in refrigerator 30 minutes.

2. Oil grid. Prepare grill for direct cooking. Soak four wooden skewers in water 20 minutes.

3. Alternately thread seitan, bell peppers, mushrooms and zucchini onto skewers.

4. Grill skewers, covered, over medium-high heat 8 minutes or until seitan is hot and glazed with sauce, brushing with some of remaining sauce and turning occasionally.

Thai-Style Pork Kabobs

Makes 4 servings

1/3 cup soy sauce

2 tablespoons lime juice

2 tablespoons water

2 teaspoons hot chili oil*

2 cloves garlic, minced

1 teaspoon minced fresh ginger

12 ounces pork tenderloin

1 red or yellow bell pepper (or a combination), cut into 1/2-inch pieces

1 red or sweet onion, cut into 1/2-inch chunks

Hot cooked rice (optional)

If hot chili oil is not available, combine 2 teaspoons vegetable oil and 1/2 teaspoon red pepper flakes in small microwavable bowl. Microwave on HIGH 30 to 45 seconds. Let stand 5 minutes to allow flavors to develop.

1. Whisk soy sauce, lime juice, water, chili oil, garlic and ginger in medium bowl until well blended. Reserve 1/3 cup in small bowl for dipping.

2. Cut pork tenderloin into 1/2-inch strips. Add to remaining soy sauce mixture in medium bowl; stir to coat. Cover and refrigerate at least 30 minutes or up to 2 hours, turning once.

3. Spray grid with nonstick cooking spray. Prepare grill for direct cooking. Soak eight 8- to 10-inch wooden skewers in water 20 minutes.

4. Remove pork from marinade; discard marinade. Alternately thread pork, bell pepper and onion onto skewers.

5. Grill kabobs, covered, over medium heat 3 to 4 minutes per side or until pork is barely pink in center. Serve with rice, if desired, and reserved dipping sauce.

Marinated Beef Brochettes

Makes 6 servings

¼ cup finely chopped onion

¼ cup olive oil

3 tablespoons lime juice

1 finely chopped seeded hot finger pepper (about 1 teaspoon)

1 clove garlic, minced

12 ounces beef tenderloin, cut into 1-inch cubes

1 medium green bell pepper, cut into 1-inch squares

1 medium red onion, cut into 1-inch pieces

1. Combine chopped onion, oil, lime juice, hot pepper and garlic in medium bowl; mix well.

2. Combine beef and marinade in large resealable food storage bag. Seal bag; turn to coat. Refrigerate 2 hours or overnight.

3. Prepare grill for direct cooking. Soak six 8-inch wooden skewers in water 20 minutes.

4. Remove beef from marinade; discard marinade. Alternately thread beef, bell pepper and red onion pieces onto skewers.

5. Grill brochettes 2 to 3 minutes per side or until desired doneness.

Spiced Chicken Skewers with Yogurt-Tahini Sauce

Makes 4 servings

1 cup plain Greek yogurt

¼ cup chopped fresh parsley, plus additional for garnish

¼ cup tahini

2 tablespoons lemon juice

1 clove garlic

¾ teaspoon salt, divided

1 tablespoon vegetable oil

2 teaspoons garam masala

1 pound boneless skinless chicken breasts, cut into 1-inch pieces

1. Spray grid with nonstick cooking spray. Prepare grill for direct cooking. Soak eight 6-inch wooden skewers in water 20 minutes.

2. Combine yogurt, ¼ cup parsley, tahini, lemon juice, garlic and ¼ teaspoon salt in food processor or blender; process until smooth. Set aside.

3. Combine oil, garam masala and remaining ½ teaspoon salt in medium bowl; mix well. Add chicken; stir to coat.

4. Thread chicken onto skewers.

5. Grill skewers over medium-high heat 5 minutes per side or until chicken is no longer pink. Serve with yogurt sauce; garnish with additional parsley.

Pork and Plum Kabobs

Makes 4 servings

3/4 pound boneless pork loin chops (1 inch thick), trimmed and cut into 1-inch pieces

1 1/2 teaspoons ground cumin

1/2 teaspoon ground cinnamon

1/4 teaspoon salt

1/4 teaspoon garlic powder

1/4 teaspoon ground red pepper

1/4 cup sliced green onions

1/4 cup raspberry fruit spread

1 tablespoon orange juice

3 plums or nectarines, pitted and cut into wedges

1. Place pork in large resealable food storage bag. Combine cumin, cinnamon, salt, garlic powder and ground red pepper in small bowl; mix well. Add to bag; seal bag and shake to coat.

2. Combine green onions, fruit spread and orange juice in medium bowl; mix well.

3. Oil grid. Prepare grill for direct cooking. Soak eight wooden skewers in water 20 minutes.

4. Alternately thread pork and plum wedges onto skewers.

5. Grill kabobs over medium heat 6 to 7 minutes per side or until pork is barely pink in center. Brush frequently with raspberry mixture during last 5 minutes of grilling.

Tofu Satay with Peanut Sauce

Makes 4 servings

Satay

- 1 package (14 ounces) firm tofu, drained and pressed*
- 1/3 cup water
- 1/3 cup soy sauce
- 1 tablespoon sesame oil
- 1 teaspoon minced garlic
- 1 teaspoon minced fresh ginger
- 1 package (8 ounces) mushrooms, trimmed
- 1 red bell pepper, cut into 1-inch pieces

Peanut Sauce

- 1 can (14 ounces) unsweetened coconut milk
- 1/2 cup creamy peanut butter
- 2 tablespoons packed brown sugar
- 1 tablespoon rice vinegar
- 1 to 2 teaspoons red Thai curry paste

Place tofu on paper towels in a colander in the sink. Place a small, flat plate on top of tofu and weigh down with a large can. Let stand 30 minutes.

1. Cut tofu into 24 cubes. Combine water, soy sauce, sesame oil, garlic and ginger in small bowl; mix well. Place tofu, mushrooms and bell pepper in large resealable food storage bag. Add soy sauce mixture; seal bag and turn gently to coat. Marinate 30 minutes, turning occasionally. Soak eight 8-inch bamboo skewers in water 20 minutes.

2. Preheat oven to 400°F. Spray 13×9-inch glass baking dish with nonstick cooking spray.

3. Drain tofu mixture; discard marinade. Thread skewers, alternating tofu with mushrooms and bell pepper. Place skewers in prepared baking dish.

4. Bake 25 minutes or until tofu is lightly browned and vegetables are softened.

5. Meanwhile, whisk coconut milk, peanut butter, brown sugar, vinegar and curry paste in small saucepan over medium heat. Bring to a boil, stirring constantly. Immediately reduce heat to low; cook about 20 minutes or until creamy and thick, stirring frequently. Serve satay with sauce.

Sweet and Sour Glazed Beef Kabobs

Makes 6 servings

3/4 cup cola beverage, divided

1/2 cup pineapple juice

1/4 cup soy sauce

1/3 cup cider vinegar

1 tablespoon Worcestershire sauce

1 tablespoon tomato paste

4 tablespoons packed dark brown sugar, divided

1 tablespoon garlic powder

1/2 teaspoon red pepper flakes

2 pounds boneless sirloin steak, cut into 1 1/2-inch pieces

1 large onion, cut into 1-inch pieces

2 1/2 teaspoons cornstarch

2 to 3 teaspoons chili-garlic sauce*

Salt and black pepper

Hot cooked rice (optional)

Chili-garlic sauce can be found in the Asian section of the supermarket.

1. Combine 1/2 cup cola, pineapple juice, soy sauce, vinegar, Worcestershire sauce, tomato paste, 2 tablespoons brown sugar, garlic powder and red pepper flakes in medium bowl; mix well.

2. Combine steak and onion in large resealable food storage bag. Add cola mixture to bag; seal bag and turn to coat. Marinate steak and onion in refrigerator overnight.

3. Remove steak and onion from marinade. Pour marinade into small saucepan; bring to a boil over high heat. Stir 2 tablespoons hot marinade into cornstarch in small bowl until smooth. Pour cornstarch mixture back into saucepan with remaining 2 tablespoons brown sugar and chili-garlic sauce. Reduce heat to medium; cook 15 to 18 minutes or until sauce is thickened and reduced to 1 cup, stirring occasionally. Season with salt and black pepper.

4. Meanwhile, preheat broiler. Line broiler pan or baking sheet with foil. Soak six wooden skewers in water 20 minutes.

5. Alternately thread steak and onion onto skewers. Place kabobs on prepared broiler pan.

6. Broil kabobs 3 minutes; turn and broil 2 minutes. Brush kabobs generously with sauce. Serve with rice, if desired.

Birthday
Cake in a Jar
page 128

Lots of Layers

Use small jars, drinking glasses, wine glasses, glass mugs or even shot glasses to make irresistible single-serving layered desserts. Brownies, cakes, cookies, fruit, pudding, ice cream and whipped cream can all be used to create fun and festive layered desserts—the possibilities are endlessly delicious!

Creamy Banana Parfait

Makes 4 servings

1 container (6 ounces) vanilla yogurt

2 ounces cream cheese, softened

1¼ cups milk

¼ teaspoon vanilla

1 package (4-serving size) instant vanilla pudding and pie filling mix

⅛ teaspoon ground nutmeg

1 ripe medium banana, very thinly sliced

½ cup (about 12) vanilla wafers, crushed

¼ cup thawed frozen whipped topping

1. Combine yogurt and cream cheese in medium bowl; beat with electric mixer at medium speed until smooth. Gradually add milk and vanilla; beat until smooth. Add pudding mix and nutmeg; beat until well blended.

2. Spoon pudding mixture into each of four wine or parfait glasses. Top with banana slices; sprinkle with cookie crumbs. (Cover bananas evenly with cookie crumbs to prevent discoloration.)

3. Cover parfaits with plastic wrap. Refrigerate at least 1 hour or up to 4 hours before serving.

4. Top each parfait with 2 tablespoons whipped topping.

Brownie Ice Cream Treats

Makes 8 servings

½ cup all-purpose flour

½ teaspoon salt

¼ teaspoon baking powder

6 tablespoons (¾ stick) butter

1 cup sugar

½ cup unsweetened Dutch process cocoa powder

2 eggs

½ teaspoon vanilla

8 (2¼-inch) jars with lids

2 cups pistachio or favorite flavor ice cream, slightly softened

Hot fudge topping, heated (optional)

1. Preheat oven to 350°F. Spray 9-inch square baking pan with nonstick cooking spray.

2. Combine flour, salt and baking powder in small bowl; mix well. Melt butter in medium saucepan over low heat. Stir in sugar until well blended. Stir in cocoa until blended. Add eggs, one at a time, beating until blended after each addition. Stir in vanilla. Stir in flour mixture until blended. Pour batter into prepared pan.

3. Bake about 20 minutes or until toothpick inserted into center comes out with fudgy crumbs. Cool completely in pan on wire rack.

4. For 2¼-inch-wide jars, cut out 16 brownies using 2-inch round cookie or biscuit cutter. (See Tip.) Remove brownie scraps from pan (any pieces left between round cut-outs); crumble into small pieces.

5. Place one brownie in each of eight ½-cup jars. Top with 2 tablespoons ice cream, pressing to form flat layer over brownie. Repeat brownie and ice cream layers.

6. Drizzle with hot fudge topping, if desired, and sprinkle with brownie crumbs. Serve immediately or make ahead through step 5, cover and freeze until ready to serve.

Tip: Measure the diameter of your jar first and cut out your brownies slightly smaller to fit in the jar. If your jar is not tall enough to fit two brownie layers, cut the brownies in half horizontally with a serrated knife.

Apple Trifle in a Jar

Makes 6 servings

1 cup milk

1 tablespoon cornstarch

2 eggs

3 tablespoons packed dark brown sugar

1 tablespoon butter

$1/8$ teaspoon salt

1 teaspoon vanilla

$1/2$ teaspoon rum extract

$1/2$ cup apple cider, divided

$1/4$ cup raisins

1 teaspoon ground cinnamon

2 cups peeled and chopped Fuji apples (2 apples)

$1/2$ angel food cake, cut into cubes, divided

1. Combine milk and cornstarch in small, heavy saucepan; stir until cornstarch is completely dissolved. Add eggs, brown sugar, butter and salt; mix well. Bring to a boil over medium-low heat; cook about 5 minutes or until thickened, whisking constantly. Remove from heat; stir in vanilla and rum extract. Set custard aside to cool completely.

2. Combine $1/4$ cup apple cider, raisins and cinnamon in medium saucepan; bring to a boil over medium-low heat. Add apple; cook until apple is fork-tender and all liquid has been absorbed, stirring frequently. Remove from heat; set aside to cool.

3. Place cake cubes in medium bowl. Sprinkle with remaining $1/4$ cup apple cider; toss to coat.

4. Place $1/4$ cup cake cubes in each of six 1-pint jars. Spoon custard mixture over cake; top with apple mixture. Repeat layers. Refrigerate until ready to serve.

Key Lime Minis

Makes 4 servings

6 whole graham crackers

2 tablespoons butter, melted

Pinch salt

1 tablespoon whipping cream or milk

1 can (14 ounces) sweetened condensed milk

6 tablespoons key lime juice

3 egg yolks

1 drop *each* yellow and green food coloring

Whipped cream

Lime slices (optional)

1. Place graham crackers in food processor; pulse until coarse crumbs form. Add butter, salt and whipping cream; pulse until well blended.

2. Whisk sweetened condensed milk, lime juice, egg yolks and food coloring in medium saucepan until well blended. Cook over medium-low heat 5 to 7 minutes, whisking frequently. Remove from heat; cool 10 minutes.

3. Press 2 heaping tablespoons crumb mixture into bottom of four $1/2$-pint jars; top evenly with lime custard. Cover and refrigerate overnight.

4. Just before serving, top with whipped cream and garnish with lime slices.

S'mores in a Jar

Makes 8 servings

Crust

- 1 sleeve honey graham crackers (9 whole crackers)
- 1/4 cup (1/2 stick) butter, melted
- 1/4 teaspoon salt

Chocolate Mousse

- 1 cup semisweet chocolate chips
- 2 cups chilled whipping cream, divided
- 4 egg yolks
- Pinch salt
- 1 teaspoon vanilla
- 1/4 cup sugar

Marshmallow Topping

- 1 jar (7 ounces) marshmallow creme
- 1 cup mini marshmallows

1. For crust, place graham crackers in food processor; process until coarse crumbs form. Add butter and 1/4 teaspoon salt; process until well blended. Press 2 tablespoons mixture into bottom of eight wide-mouth 1/2-pint jars. Freeze 10 minutes.

2. For mousse, heat chocolate chips in medium saucepan over low heat until melted, stirring frequently. Remove from heat; stir in 1/4 cup whipping cream.

3. Combine egg yolks and pinch of salt in medium bowl. Whisk about half of chocolate mixture into egg yolks; whisk egg yolk mixture back into chocolate mixture in saucepan. Cook over low heat 2 minutes, whisking constantly. Remove from heat; cool 5 minutes.

4. Beat remaining 1 3/4 cups whipping cream and vanilla in medium bowl with electric mixer at medium-high speed until soft peaks form. Gradually add sugar; beat until stiff peaks form. Stir about one fourth of whipped cream into chocolate mixture; fold chocolate mixture into remaining whipped cream until completely blended.

5. Spoon heaping spoonful of marshmallow creme on top of crust in each jar; press into even layer with dampened hands. Top with heaping 1/4 cup mousse.

6. Preheat broiler. Line small baking pan with foil; spray with nonstick cooking spray. Spread marshmallows in prepared pan. Broil about 30 seconds or until marshmallows are toasted. Scoop toasted marshmallows on top of each serving.

Strawberry Cheesecake Parfaits

Makes 4 servings

1½ cups vanilla
    Greek yogurt

½ cup whipped cream
    cheese, at room
    temperature

2 tablespoons
    powdered sugar

1 teaspoon vanilla

2 cups sliced fresh
    strawberries

2 teaspoons
    granulated sugar

8 honey graham
    cracker squares,
    coarsely crumbled
    (about 2 cups)

Fresh mint leaves
(optional)

1. Whisk yogurt, cream cheese, powdered sugar and vanilla in small bowl until smooth and well blended.

2. Combine strawberries and granulated sugar in small bowl; toss gently.

3. Layer ¼ cup yogurt mixture, ¼ cup strawberries and ¼ cup graham cracker crumbs in each of four glasses or dessert dishes. Repeat layers. Garnish with mint. Serve immediately.

Birthday Cake in a Jar

Makes 20 servings

Cake

- 2 cups all-purpose flour
- 4 teaspoons baking powder
- 1/2 teaspoon salt
- 1 1/2 cups granulated sugar
- 1/2 cup (1 stick) butter, softened
- 1 cup milk
- 1 teaspoon vanilla
- 3 eggs
- 1/2 cup rainbow sprinkles

Frosting

- 1/2 cup (1 stick) butter, softened
- 3 cups powdered sugar
- 3 tablespoons whipping cream
- 1/2 teaspoon vanilla

Garnishes

- Additional sprinkles
- Ice cream
- Chocolate ice cream topping

1. For cake, preheat oven to 350°F. Spray jelly-roll pan with nonstick cooking spray; line with parchment paper.

2. Sift flour, baking powder and salt into large bowl. Stir in granulated sugar. Add 1/2 cup butter, milk and 1 teaspoon vanilla; beat with electric mixer at low speed 30 seconds. Beat at medium speed 2 minutes. Add eggs; beat 2 minutes or until well blended. Fold in 1/2 cup sprinkles. Pour batter into prepared pan.

3. Bake 18 to 20 minutes or until toothpick inserted into center comes out clean. Cool completely in pan on wire rack.

4. For frosting, beat 1/2 cup butter in large bowl with electric mixer at medium speed 30 seconds or until creamy. Gradually add powdered sugar alternately with cream; beating until well blended. Add 1/2 teaspoon vanilla; beat at medium-high speed until light and fluffy.

5. Cut cake in half crosswise. Spread half of frosting over bottom half of cake; top with remaining half of cake. Spread remaining frosting over cake; top with additional sprinkles.

6. Cut cake into circles or squares that will fit into 1-pint jars. Place one cake circle in each jar; top with scoop of ice cream, chocolate topping and additional sprinkles.

Double Chocolate Cookies and Cream Mousse

Makes 8 servings

8 ounces semisweet chocolate, chopped

2½ cups chilled whipping cream, divided

4 egg yolks

Pinch salt

1¼ teaspoons vanilla, divided

¼ cup granulated sugar

23 chocolate sandwich cookies, divided

1 tablespoon powdered sugar

1. Melt chocolate in medium saucepan over very low heat, stirring frequently. Remove from heat; stir in ¼ cup cream until well blended.

2. Whisk egg yolks and pinch of salt in medium bowl. Whisk about half of chocolate mixture into egg yolks until blended; whisk egg yolk mixture back into chocolate mixture in saucepan. Cook over low heat 2 minutes, whisking constantly. Remove from heat; cool to room temperature.

3. Beat 1¾ cups cream and 1 teaspoon vanilla in large bowl with electric mixer at high speed until soft peaks form. Gradually beat in granulated sugar; continue beating until stiff peaks form. Fold about one fourth of whipped cream into chocolate mixture; fold chocolate mixture into remaining whipped cream until completely combined.

4. Finely chop 2 cookies; fold into mousse. Coarsely chop 2 cookies for topping. Cut remaining 19 cookies into quarters; set aside. Refrigerate mousse 4 hours or overnight.

5. Beat remaining ½ cup cream in medium bowl with electric mixer at high speed 30 seconds or until thickened. Add powdered sugar and remaining ¼ teaspoon vanilla; beat until stiff peaks form.

6. Spoon ¼ cup mousse into each of eight wide-mouth ½-pint jars. Top with ¼ cup quartered cookies and another ¼ cup mousse. Garnish with dollop of sweetened whipped cream and chopped cookies.

Berry Shortcake Trifles

Makes 4 servings

Lemon Curd

1 cup granulated sugar

$^1/_2$ cup (1 stick) butter

$^2/_3$ cup lemon juice

1 tablespoon grated lemon peel

$^1/_4$ teaspoon salt

4 eggs, beaten

Berries

8 ounces fresh strawberries, stemmed and diced

8 ounces fresh blueberries

$^1/_3$ cup granulated sugar

Whipped Cream

4 ounces cream cheese, softened

6 tablespoons powdered sugar, divided

1 cup whipping cream, divided

$^1/_4$ teaspoon vanilla

1 prepared pound cake (about 14 ounces), cut into $^1/_2$-inch cubes

1. For lemon curd, combine 1 cup granulated sugar, butter, lemon juice, lemon peel and salt in medium saucepan; cook and stir over medium heat until butter is melted and sugar is dissolved. Gradually whisk in eggs in thin, steady stream. Cook over medium-low heat 5 minutes or until thickened to the consistency of pudding, whisking constantly. Strain through fine-mesh sieve into medium bowl. Press plastic wrap onto surface; refrigerate at least 2 hours or until cold.

2. Meanwhile, combine strawberries, blueberries and $^1/_3$ cup granulated sugar in medium bowl; stir gently to blend. Cover and refrigerate at least 2 hours.

3. Beat cream cheese, 3 tablespoons powdered sugar, 2 tablespoons whipping cream and vanilla in large bowl with electric mixer at medium speed 3 minutes or until smooth.

4. Beat remaining whipping cream and 3 tablespoons powdered sugar in separate medium bowl with electric mixer at high speed until stiff peaks form. Fold into cream cheese mixture until well blended.

5. Drain berries, reserving juice. Place $^1/_2$ cup pound cake cubes in each of four wide-mouth 1-pint jars. Sprinkle cake cubes in each jar with 3 teaspoons reserved berry juice; top with scant $^1/_4$ cup whipped cream, 2 tablespoons lemon curd and 1 tablespoon berries. Repeat layers. Refrigerate overnight.

Cherry Parfait Crunch

Makes 8 servings

1½ pounds dark or light sweet cherries

1 cup unsweetened apple juice

½ teaspoon ground cinnamon

Dash ground nutmeg

2 tablespoons water

2 teaspoons cornstarch

⅔ cup natural wheat and barley cereal or granola

½ cup chopped toasted almonds*

4 cups vanilla yogurt

*To toast almonds, cook in small skillet over medium heat 3 minutes or until lightly browned, stirring frequently.

1. Remove stems and pits from cherries; cut into halves (about 4½ cups).

2. Combine cherries, apple juice, cinnamon and nutmeg in small saucepan; cook and stir over medium heat 5 minutes or until cherries begin to soften.

3. Whisk water into cornstarch in small bowl until smooth; stir into saucepan. Cook and stir over high heat until mixture boils and thickens slightly. Let cool 10 minutes; cover and refrigerate until cold.

4. Combine cereal and almonds in small bowl. Layer half of cherry mixture, half of yogurt and half of cereal mixture in eight wine or parfait glasses; repeat layers.

Brownie Layer Dessert in a Jar

Makes 6 servings

1 package (19 to 21 ounces) chocolate brownie mix, plus ingredients to prepare mix

1 package (4-serving size) chocolate instant pudding mix, plus ingredients to prepare mix

2 cups powdered sugar

1 package (4 ounces) cream cheese, softened

1 to 2 teaspoons milk

¼ teaspoon vanilla

1 cup mini chocolate chips

½ (8-ounce) container frozen whipped topping, thawed

1. Prepare brownie mix according to package directions for 13×9-inch pan. Cool completely.

2. Prepare pudding mix according to package directions; set aside.

3. Combine powdered sugar, cream cheese, milk and vanilla in medium bowl; beat with electric mixer at medium speed 1 to 2 minutes or until creamy. Fold in chocolate chips.

4. Cut cooled brownies into 12 (2½-inch) circles (or fit size of jar). Place one brownie circle into each of six 1-pint jars; top each with ¼ cup cream cheese mixture, ½ cup pudding, another brownie circle and whipped topping. Refrigerate until ready to serve.

Bittersweet
Chocolate
Raspberry
Cupcakes
page 154

Personal Desserts

Who wouldn't want their own personal sweet treat? Cookies and cupcakes are easy options when it comes to individual portions, but mini cakes and pies also make perfect party food.

Tiny Peanut Butter Sandwiches

Makes 6 to 7 dozen sandwiches

1¼ cups all-purpose flour

½ teaspoon baking powder

½ teaspoon baking soda

¼ teaspoon salt

½ cup (1 stick) butter, softened

½ cup granulated sugar

½ cup packed brown sugar

½ cup creamy peanut butter

1 egg

1 teaspoon vanilla

1 cup semisweet chocolate chips

½ cup whipping cream

1. Preheat oven to 350°F. Combine flour, baking powder, baking soda and salt in medium bowl; mix well.

2. Beat butter, granulated sugar and brown sugar in large bowl with electric mixer at medium speed until light and fluffy. Beat in peanut butter, egg and vanilla until well blended. Gradually add flour mixture; beat at low speed until blended.

3. Shape dough by ½ teaspoonfuls into balls; place 1 inch apart on ungreased cookie sheets. Flatten balls slightly in criss-cross pattern with fork.

4. Bake 6 minutes or just until set. Cool on cookie sheets 4 minutes; remove to wire racks to cool completely.

5. For filling, place chocolate chips in medium bowl. Place cream in small microwavable bowl; microwave on HIGH 2 minutes or just until simmering. Pour over chocolate chips; let stand 2 minutes. Stir until smooth. Let stand 10 minutes or until filling thickens to desired consistency.

6. Spread scant teaspoon filling on flat side of half of cookies; top with remaining cookies. Store in airtight container.

Salted Caramel Cupcakes

Makes 12 cupcakes

1 1/2 cups all-purpose flour

1 teaspoon baking powder

1/2 teaspoon salt

1 cup packed brown sugar

1/2 cup (1 stick) butter, softened

2 eggs

1 teaspoon vanilla

1/2 cup buttermilk

Salted Caramel Frosting (recipe follows)

Flaky sea salt

1. Preheat oven to 325°F. Line 12 standard (2 1/2-inch) muffin cups with paper baking cups. Combine flour, baking powder and 1/2 teaspoon salt in small bowl; mix well.

2. Beat brown sugar and butter in large bowl with electric mixer at medium speed until fluffy. Add eggs and vanilla; beat until well blended. Add flour mixture and buttermilk; beat just until combined. Spoon batter evenly into prepared muffin cups.

3. Bake 20 to 25 minutes or until toothpick inserted into centers comes out clean. Cool in pan 10 minutes; remove to wire rack to cool completely.

4. Prepare Salted Caramel Frosting. Pipe or spread frosting on cupcakes; sprinkle lightly with flaky salt.

Salted Caramel Frosting

Makes about 2 1/2 cups

1/2 cup granulated sugar

2 tablespoons water

1/4 cup whipping cream

1 teaspoon sea salt

1 cup (2 sticks) butter, softened

2 1/2 cups powdered sugar

1. Heat granulated sugar and water in heavy medium saucepan over high heat; cook, without stirring, until medium to dark amber in color. Remove from heat; carefully stir in cream and sea salt (mixture will foam). Set aside to cool 15 minutes.

2. Beat butter and caramel mixture in large bowl with electric mixer at medium-high speed until well blended. Add powdered sugar; beat until thick and creamy. (If frosting is too soft, refrigerate 10 minutes before piping or spreading on cupcakes.)

Mini Black and White Cheesecakes

Makes 12 servings

1 cup chocolate wafer cookie crumbs

12 ounces cream cheese, softened

1/2 cup sugar

2 teaspoons vanilla

1/2 cup milk

2 eggs

1/2 cup semisweet chocolate chips, melted and slightly cooled

1. Preheat oven to 325°F. Line 12 standard (2½-inch) muffin cups with paper baking cups. Spoon rounded tablespoon of cookie crumbs into each cup.

2. Beat cream cheese, sugar and vanilla in large bowl with electric mixer at medium speed until light and fluffy. Add milk and eggs; beat until well blended. Transfer half of mixture to medium bowl. Stir in melted chocolate until well blended.

3. Divide remaining plain cream cheese mixture evenly among prepared muffin cups. Bake 10 minutes.

4. Divide chocolate mixture evenly among muffin cups; spread to edges. Bake 15 minutes or until centers are almost set. Cool completely in pan on wire rack. Store in refrigerator.

Cranberry Phyllo Cheesecake Tarts

Makes 12 servings

1 cup fresh or frozen cranberries

1/4 cup plus 1 tablespoon sugar, divided

2 tablespoons orange juice

1 teaspoon grated orange peel

1/4 teaspoon ground allspice

6 sheets phyllo dough (14×9-inch sheets), thawed

1 container (8 ounces) whipped cream cheese

8 ounces vanilla yogurt

1 teaspoon vanilla

1. Preheat oven to 350°F. Combine cranberries, 1/4 cup sugar, orange juice, orange peel and allspice in small saucepan; cook and stir over medium heat until berries pop and mixture thickens. Set aside to cool completely.

2. Lightly spray 12 standard (2 1/2-inch) muffin cups with butter-flavored nonstick cooking spray. Cut phyllo dough in half lengthwise, then crosswise into thirds.

3. Spray one phyllo square lightly with cooking spray. Top with second square, slightly offsetting corners; spray lightly with cooking spray. Top with third square. Place phyllo stack in one prepared muffin cup, pressing into bottom and up side of cup. Repeat with remaining phyllo squares.

4. Bake 3 to 4 minutes or until golden brown. Cool completely in pan on wire rack.

5. Beat cream cheese, yogurt, remaining 1 tablespoon sugar and vanilla in medium bowl with electric mixer at medium speed until smooth. Divide mixture evenly among phyllo cups; top with cranberry mixture.

Plum-Side Down Cakes

Makes 8 servings

2 tablespoons butter

3 tablespoons packed brown sugar

3 plums, sliced

1/2 cup granulated sugar

2 tablespoons shortening

1 egg

1 cup all-purpose flour

1 teaspoon baking powder

1/4 teaspoon salt

1/3 cup milk

1. Preheat oven to 350°F. Spray eight standard (2½-inch) muffin cups with nonstick cooking spray.

2. Place butter in small microwavable bowl; microwave on LOW (30%) just until melted. Stir in brown sugar until blended. Spoon evenly into prepared muffin cups. Arrange plum slices in bottom of each cup.

3. Beat granulated sugar and shortening in medium bowl with electric mixer at medium speed until fluffy. Beat in egg until well blended.

4. Combine flour, baking powder and salt in small bowl; mix well. Add to shortening mixture; beat until blended. Add milk; beat until smooth. Spoon batter into prepared muffin cups, filling three-fourths full. Place pan on baking sheet.

5. Bake 20 to 22 minutes or until toothpick inserted into centers comes out clean. Cool in pan 10 minutes. Run knife around each cup; invert onto wire rack to cool completely.

Marshmallow Sandwich Cookies

Makes about 2 dozen sandwich cookies

2 cups all-purpose flour

1/2 cup unsweetened cocoa powder

2 teaspoons baking soda

1/2 teaspoon salt

1 1/2 cups sugar, divided

2/3 cup butter, softened

1/4 cup light corn syrup

1 egg

1 teaspoon vanilla

24 large marshmallows

1. Preheat oven to 350°F. Combine flour, cocoa, baking soda and salt in medium bowl; mix well.

2. Beat 1 1/4 cups sugar and butter in large bowl with electric mixer at medium-high speed until light and fluffy. Beat in corn syrup, egg and vanilla until blended. Add flour mixture; beat at low speed until blended. Cover and refrigerate 15 minutes or until dough is firm enough to shape into balls.

3. Place remaining 1/4 cup sugar in small bowl. Shape dough into 1-inch balls; roll in sugar to coat. Place cookies 3 inches apart on ungreased cookie sheets.

4. Bake 10 to 11 minutes or until set. Cool on cookie sheets 3 minutes; remove to wire racks to cool completely.

5. Place one cookie on microwavable plate; top with one marshmallow. Microwave on HIGH about 10 seconds or until marshmallow is softened. Immediately place another cookie, flat side down, on top of hot marshmallow; press together. Repeat with remaining cookies and marshmallows.

Individual Blueberry Pies

Makes 6 servings

1 package (15 ounces) refrigerated pie crusts (2 crusts)

4 cups fresh or frozen blueberries

$\frac{1}{4}$ cup sugar, plus additional for topping

$\frac{1}{4}$ cup all-purpose flour

2 teaspoons lemon peel

$\frac{1}{2}$ teaspoon vanilla

$\frac{1}{2}$ teaspoon ground cinnamon

2 tablespoons butter, cut into small pieces

1 egg

1 teaspoon water

1. Preheat oven to 375°F. Spray six ovenproof jars, mugs or ramekins with nonstick cooking spray.

2. Cut each pie crust into six equal pieces. Press one piece into bottom of each prepared jar.

3. Combine blueberries, $\frac{1}{4}$ cup sugar, flour, lemon peel, vanilla and cinnamon in medium bowl; toss gently to coat. Spoon mixture over crusts in jars; dot with butter.

4. Cut remaining six pieces of dough into $\frac{1}{2}$-inch strips. Arrange strips in lattice design over top of each jar; press ends of strips securely to seal. Beat egg and water in small bowl; brush over lattice. Sprinkle with additional sugar. Place jars on baking sheet.

5. Bake 40 to 45 minutes or until crusts are golden brown. Let stand 10 to 15 minutes before serving.

Bittersweet Chocolate Raspberry Cupcakes

Makes 20 cupcakes

1¹/₂ cups all-purpose flour

1 teaspoon baking soda

1 teaspoon baking powder

¹/₂ teaspoon salt

³/₄ cup hot coffee

³/₄ cup unsweetened cocoa powder

8 ounces bittersweet chocolate, chopped, divided

1¹/₄ cups sugar

2 eggs

¹/₃ cup vegetable oil

1 teaspoon vanilla

³/₄ cup buttermilk

2 pints fresh raspberries, divided

¹/₂ cup whipping cream

1. Preheat oven to 350°F. Line 20 standard (2¹/₂-inch) muffin cups with paper baking cups.

2. Combine flour, baking soda, baking powder and salt in small bowl; mix well. Combine coffee, cocoa and 2 ounces chopped chocolate in large bowl; whisk until chocolate is melted and mixture is smooth. Stir in sugar, eggs, oil and vanilla until well blended. Add flour mixture alternately with buttermilk, stirring until blended after each addition. Spoon batter evenly into prepared muffin cups; place three raspberries in each cup.

3. Bake 22 minutes or until toothpick inserted into centers comes out clean. Cool in pans 5 minutes; remove to wire racks to cool completely.

4. Meanwhile, place remaining 6 ounces chopped chocolate in medium bowl. Heat cream to a simmer in small saucepan over medium heat or in microwave. Pour cream over chocolate; let stand 2 minutes. Whisk until melted and smooth.

5. Dip tops of cupcakes in chocolate mixture; return to wire racks. Top with raspberries. Let stand until set.

Upside Down Peach Cornbread Cakes

Makes 8 servings

1/4 cup (1/2 stick) butter

1/2 cup packed brown sugar

1 fresh peach, thinly sliced

2 packages (8 1/2 ounces each) corn bread mix

2 eggs

1/2 cup milk

2 tablespoons vegetable oil

1 3/4 cups diced fresh peaches or frozen diced unsweetened peaches, thawed

1. Preheat oven to 400°F. Spray eight standard (2 1/2-inch) muffin cups or ramekins with nonstick cooking spray.

2. Place 1/2 tablespoon butter and 1 tablespoon brown sugar in bottom of each prepared muffin cup. Divide peach slices evenly among muffin cups.

3. Whisk corn bread mix, eggs, milk and oil in large bowl until well blended. Stir in diced peaches. Pour 3/4 cup batter into each cup.

4. Bake 20 minutes or until golden brown and toothpick inserted into centers comes out clean. Cool in pan 5 minutes. Run knife around edges; invert cakes onto serving plate.

Serving Suggestion: Serve with vanilla ice cream or whipped cream.

Mini Tartes Tatin

Makes 6 servings

5 small sweet-tart apples such as Pink Lady or Honeycrisp,* peeled, cored and sliced crosswise into ⅛-inch-thick rounds

2 tablespoons granulated sugar

1 teaspoon ground cinnamon

3 tablespoons butter

2 tablespoons packed brown sugar

1 refrigerated pie crust (half of 15-ounce package)

Whipped cream (optional)

*Look for apples that are about the size of standard muffin pan cups, about 2 to 2½ inches in diameter and 5 to 6 ounces each.

1. Preheat oven to 350°F. Spray six standard (2½-inch) nonstick muffin cups with nonstick cooking spray.

2. Combine apple slices, granulated sugar and cinnamon in large bowl; toss to coat.

3. Place ½ tablespoon butter in each prepared muffin cup. Top with 1 teaspoon brown sugar, spreading to cover bottom of cup. Stack apple slices in cups, packing down to fit; fill center holes with broken or small apple slices. (Stacks will be tall and extend about 1 inch above rim of cup.) Place pan on rimmed baking sheet; cover loosely with foil.

4. Bake 25 minutes (apples will sink slightly and be crisp-tender).

5. Meanwhile, let pie crust stand at room temperature 15 minutes. Unroll crust on work surface; cut out six circles with 2½- to 3-inch biscuit cutter.

6. Place one dough circle on top of each stack of apples, pressing slightly around apples. Bake, uncovered, 20 minutes or until crust is light golden brown. Cool in pan 3 minutes. Place cutting board on top of pan and invert. Carefully remove muffin pan; transfer tarts to serving platter or plates. Serve warm with whipped cream, if desired.

Strawberry Milk Shake Cupcakes

Makes 24 cupcakes

2 cups all-purpose flour

1½ cups granulated sugar

4 teaspoons baking powder

½ teaspoon salt

1¼ cups (2½ sticks) butter, softened, divided

1 cup plus 6 to 8 tablespoons milk, divided

2 teaspoons vanilla, divided

3 eggs

2 containers (7 ounces each) plain Greek yogurt

1 cup seedless strawberry preserves

6 cups powdered sugar, divided

¼ cup shortening

Pink food coloring

Assorted pastel sugar pearls and decorating sugar

1. Preheat oven to 350°F. Line 24 standard (2½-inch) muffin cups with paper baking cups.

2. Combine flour, granulated sugar, baking powder and salt in large bowl; mix well. Add ½ cup butter; beat with electric mixer at medium speed 30 seconds. Add 1 cup milk and 1 teaspoon vanilla; beat 2 minutes. Add eggs; beat 2 minutes. Spoon batter evenly into prepared muffin cups.

3. Bake 20 minutes or until toothpick inserted into centers comes out clean. Cool in pans 10 minutes; remove to wire racks to cool completely.

4. For filling, combine yogurt and preserves in medium bowl; mix well. Transfer to piping bag fitted with medium round tip. Press tip into top of each cupcake and squeeze bag to fill.

5. Beat 3 cups powdered sugar, remaining ¾ cup butter, shortening, 4 tablespoons milk and remaining 1 teaspoon vanilla in large bowl with electric mixer at low speed until smooth. Add remaining 3 cups powdered sugar; beat until light and fluffy, adding remaining milk, 1 tablespoon at a time, as needed to reach desired consistency. Add food coloring, a few drops at a time, until desired shade of pink is reached.

6. Pipe or spread frosting on cupcakes. Decorate as desired.

Molten Chocolate Cakes

Makes 8 servings

1 package (about 15 ounces) chocolate fudge cake mix

1 1/2 cups water

3 eggs

1/2 cup canola or vegetable oil

4 ounces bittersweet chocolate, chopped

4 ounces semisweet chocolate, chopped

1/2 cup whipping cream

1/4 cup (1/2 stick) butter, cut into small pieces

1 tablespoon light corn syrup

1/4 teaspoon vanilla

1/8 teaspoon salt

Caramel ice cream topping

Vanilla ice cream

1. Preheat oven to 350°F. Spray eight jumbo (3 1/2-inch) muffin cups with nonstick cooking spray.

2. Beat cake mix, water, eggs and oil in large bowl with electric mixer at low speed 30 seconds. Beat at medium speed 2 minutes. Pour 1/2 cup batter into each prepared muffin cup; discard remaining batter. Bake 25 minutes or until toothpick inserted into centers comes out clean. Cool in pan 5 minutes; remove to wire racks to cool.

3. Meanwhile, combine bittersweet chocolate, semisweet chocolate, cream, butter, corn syrup, vanilla and salt in medium microwavable bowl; microwave on HIGH 30 seconds. Stir; microwave at additional 30-second intervals until chocolate begins to melt. Whisk until smooth. Reserve 1/2 cup chocolate mixture in small microwavable bowl for topping.

4. When cakes have cooled, cut off domed top of each cake with serrated knife. Invert cakes so wider part is on the bottom. Use 1 1/2-inch biscuit cutter or small serrated knife to remove hole in top of each cake (narrow part) about 1 inch deep. Reserve cake from holes for serving.

5. Fill hole in each cake with 2 tablespoons chocolate mixture; top with reserved cake pieces. Microwave reserved 1/2 cup chocolate mixture on HIGH 20 seconds or until melted.

6. For each serving, drizzle caramel topping on microwavable plate. Arrange cake on plate; microwave on HIGH 30 seconds until chocolate filling is hot. Top with ice cream; drizzle with warm chocolate mixture.

Chocolate
Cookie Pops
page 182

Sweets on Sticks

Skewers aren't just for dinner—they're a great way to serve dessert too! In addition to frozen pops, you can use skewers or pop sticks for cookies, fruit or cubes of cake. Some of these skewered desserts can also be creatively dipped, drizzled and/or decorated for extra party pizzazz.

Chocolate Chip Angel Food Cake Kabobs with Strawberry Sauce

Makes 8 servings

1 package (16 ounces) angel food cake mix

1/3 cup mini chocolate chips

1 cup sliced fresh strawberries

1 cup sugar

1 teaspoon lemon juice

1/4 cup water

1 teaspoon cornstarch

24 small fresh strawberries

1. Preheat oven to 350°F. Prepare cake mix according to package directions; stir chocolate chips into batter. Gently spoon batter into three 8½×4½-inch loaf pans.

2. Bake 28 minutes or until golden brown. Cool completely in pans on wire racks.

3. Meanwhile, combine sliced strawberries, sugar and lemon juice in small saucepan. Whisk water into cornstarch in small bowl until smooth; stir into strawberry mixture. Bring to a boil over high heat. Reduce heat to low; cook 1 minute or until thickened, stirring constantly.*

4. Remove cooled cakes from pans; wrap and freeze two cakes for another use. Cut third cake into six slices; gently tear or cut each slice into four pieces.

5. Alternate three cake pieces and three whole strawberries on each of eight wooden skewers. Serve with Strawberry Sauce.

*Sauce may be served chunky or pureéd with hand-held immersion blender until smooth.

Frozen Polar Bear Bites

Makes 6 servings

2 medium bananas

12 pop sticks

1/2 cup creamy peanut butter

1/2 cup mini marshmallows

1/4 cup dry-roasted peanuts, chopped

2 tablespoons chocolate sprinkles

1. Cut each banana into six equal pieces. Insert tips of sticks into peanut butter, then into banana pieces. Place on waxed paper-lined baking sheet.

2. Combine marshmallows, peanuts and chocolate sprinkles in shallow dish; mix well.

3. Place peanut butter in small microwavable bowl; microwave on HIGH 20 to 30 seconds or until melted and smooth.

4. Dip each banana piece in melted peanut butter, turning to coat evenly. Roll in marshmallow mixture. Place on prepared baking sheet; let stand until set. Freeze 6 to 8 hours or until firm.

Sweet Swirly Pops

Makes about 24 pops

½ baked and cooled
   13×9-inch cake*

½ cup plus
   2 tablespoons
   frosting

½ (14- to 16-ounce)
   package chocolate
   candy coating

½ (14- to 16-ounce)
   package white
   candy coating

½ (14- to 16-ounce)
   package pink
   and/or red candy
   coating

24 lollipop sticks

   Foam block

*Prepare a cake from a
mix according to package
directions or use your
favorite recipe. Cool cake
completely before using.*

1. Line large baking sheet with waxed paper. Use hands to crumble cake into large bowl. (You should end up with fine crumbs and no large cake pieces remaining.)

2. Add frosting to cake crumbs; mix with hands until well blended. Shape mixture into 1½-inch balls (about 2 tablespoons cake mixture per ball); place on prepared baking sheet. Cover with plastic wrap; refrigerate at least 1 hour or freeze 10 minutes to firm.

3. When cake balls are firm, place candy coatings in separate deep microwavable bowls. Melt according to package directions. Dip one lollipop stick about ½ inch into melted coating; insert stick into cake ball (no more than halfway through). Return cake pop to baking sheet in refrigerator to set. Repeat with remaining cake balls and sticks.

4. Working with one cake pop at a time, hold stick and dip cake ball into melted chocolate or white coating to cover completely, letting excess coating drip off. Rotate stick gently and/or tap stick on edge of bowl, if necessary, to remove excess coating.

5. Immediately drizzle cake pop with melted pink or red coating using fork or spoon, turning pop constantly while drizzling. (For swirls to set smoothly in base coating, pop must be turned or shaken while drizzling, and drizzling must be done while base coating is still wet.) Place cake pop in foam block to set.

Tip: To make cake pops with two color swirls, drizzle cake pop with both colors immediately after dipping in base coating as directed in step 5.

Margarita Pops

Makes 8 pops

2 cups water

²/₃ cup lime juice
(3 to 4 limes)

½ cup tequila

¼ cup sugar

2 tablespoons
Triple Sec or
orange liqueur

8 (2-ounce) plastic
or paper cups
or shot glasses

8 pop sticks

Coarse salt

1. Combine water, lime juice, tequila, sugar and Triple Sec in small saucepan; bring to a boil over medium heat. Boil 1 minute or until sugar is dissolved, stirring constantly. Remove from heat; cool to room temperature.

2. Pour mixture into cups. Cover top of each cup with small piece of foil. Freeze 2 hours.

3. Insert sticks through center of foil. Freeze 3 hours or until firm.

4. Remove foil and gently twist frozen pops out of plastic cups or peel away paper cups.*

5. Spread coarse salt on small plate. Roll pops in coarse salt. Serve immediately or place in plastic cups and return to freezer until ready to serve.

If using shot glasses, place bottoms of glasses under cool running water until loosened. (Do not twist or pull sticks.) Or run a small thin knife around the inside edge of glasses to release pops.

Chocolate-Covered Espresso Pops

Makes 24 pops

1 container (about 9 ounces) chocolate sprinkles

1 pint (2 cups) chocolate ice cream or gelato

1 cup chocolate-covered espresso beans, coarsely chopped*

24 pop sticks

Chocolate-covered espresso beans are available in fine supermarkets and gourmet food stores.

1. Line medium baking sheet with plastic wrap. Spread chocolate sprinkles in shallow dish; set aside.

2. Scoop gelato into chilled large metal bowl. Cut in chocolate-covered espresso beans with pastry blender or two knives; fold and cut again. Repeat, working quickly, until mixture is evenly incorporated.

3. Scoop 24 rounded tablespoonfuls ice cream mixture into sprinkles. Gently roll into balls, turning to coat and pressing sprinkles evenly into gelato. Place on prepared baking sheet. Freeze 1 hour.

4. Insert sticks. Freeze 1 hour or until firm.

Tip: Use coffee stirrers for the pop sticks to add a pop of color and make these frozen treats more fun!

Strawberry Lemonade Pops

Makes 6 pops

½ (12-ounce) can frozen lemonade concentrate, partially thawed

1 cup ice cubes

½ cup sliced fresh strawberries

½ cup water

6 (3-ounce) paper or plastic cups or pop molds

6 pop sticks

1. Combine lemonade concentrate, ice cubes, strawberries and water in blender or food processor; blend until smooth.

2. Pour mixture into cups. Cover top of each cup with small piece of foil. Freeze 1 hour.

3. Insert sticks through center of foil. Freeze 4 hours or until firm.

4. To serve, remove foil and peel away paper cups or gently twist frozen pops out of plastic cups.

Frozen Chocolate Banana Pops

Makes 6 pops

3 bananas,* peeled

6 pop sticks or
wooden skewers

$1/2$ cup semisweet
chocolate chips

$1^1/2$ teaspoons
vegetable oil

$1/4$ cup sprinkles,
chopped peanuts,
coconut or crushed
cookies (optional)

*Or substitute 6 baby
bananas.*

1. Line baking sheet with waxed paper or foil. Cut each banana in half; insert stick halfway into each banana. Place on prepared baking sheet; freeze 1 hour.

2. Combine chocolate chips and oil in small saucepan; stir over low heat until melted and smooth. Place toppings on individual plates, if using.

3. Remove bananas from freezer. Spoon chocolate over each banana while holding over saucepan. Roll in toppings to coat.

4. Return pops to baking sheet; freeze about 1 hour or until chocolate and toppings are set. Store in airtight container or resealable freezer food storage bag.

Avocado Lime Pops

Makes 6 pops

1 avocado

1 cup sugar

1 cup milk

Juice and grated peel of 2 limes

¼ teaspoon vanilla

6 (5-ounce) plastic cups or paper cups or pop molds

6 pop sticks

1. Combine avocado, sugar, milk, lime juice, lime peel and vanilla in blender or food processor; blend until smooth.

2. Pour mixture into cups. Cover top of each cup with small piece of foil. Freeze 1 hour.

3. Insert sticks through center of foil. Freeze 4 hours or until firm.

4. To serve, remove foil and gently twist frozen pops out of plastic cups or peel away paper cups.

Variation: Make these plain pops more appealing by using plastic cups, which give the pops a ridged texture.

Chocolate Cookie Pops

Makes 16 pops

2 cups all-purpose flour

½ cup unsweetened cocoa powder

½ teaspoon baking powder

½ teaspoon salt

1 cup (2 sticks) butter, softened

1 cup granulated sugar, plus additional for flattening cookies

½ cup packed brown sugar

1 egg

1 teaspoon vanilla

16 pop sticks

½ cup semisweet chocolate chips

1 teaspoon shortening, divided

½ cup white chocolate chips or chopped white chocolate candy bar

Sprinkles and decors

1. Preheat oven to 350°F.

2. Combine flour, cocoa, baking powder and salt in small bowl; mix well. Beat butter, 1 cup granulated sugar and brown sugar in large bowl with electric mixer at medium speed until light and fluffy. Beat in egg and vanilla until well blended. Gradually beat in flour mixture at low speed until blended.

3. Drop dough by scant ¼ cupfuls onto ungreased or parchment-lined cookie sheets, spacing 3 inches apart. Dip bottom of glass in granulated sugar; press dough to flatten cookies until 2 inches in diameter. Insert stick 1½ inches into each cookie.

4. Bake 14 to 16 minutes or until cookies are set. Cool on cookie sheets 10 minutes. If necessary, trim uneven crispy edges from cookies with sharp knife. Remove to wire racks to cool completely.

5. Combine semisweet chocolate chips and ½ teaspoon shortening in small microwavable bowl; microwave on HIGH 30 seconds. Stir; microwave at 10-second intervals until mixture is melted and smooth. Repeat with white chocolate chips and remaining ½ teaspoon shortening. Place glazes in separate small resealable food storage bags with small corners cut off. Pipe in spiral shape on cookies; immediately sprinkle with decors. Let stand until set.

Tip: To use colorful paper straws instead of wooden pop sticks, bake cookies as directed without sticks and immediately remove to wire racks. Carefully insert a straw into each hot cookie all the way to the top. Cool completely.

Creamy Dreamy Orange Pops

Makes 8 pops

2 cups ice

1½ cups vanilla yogurt

¾ cup frozen orange juice concentrate

½ cup milk

¼ teaspoon vanilla

Pop molds with lids

1. Combine ice, yogurt, orange juice concentrate, milk and vanilla in blender or food processor; blend until smooth.

2. Pour mixture into molds. Cover with lids. Freeze 6 hours or until firm.*

3. To remove pops from molds, place bottoms of pops under warm running water until loosened. Press firmly on bottoms to release. (Do not twist or pull lids.)

If using paper or plastic cups or molds without lids, cover each cup with small piece of foil. Freeze mixture 2 hours before inserting pop sticks through center of foil.

Tip: Frozen juice concentrate is the key to simple and delicious frozen pops. Try any juice flavor and pair it with yogurt for a creamy fruity frozen treat.

Tiny Toffee Pops

Makes 14 pops

1 pint chocolate
   ice cream

1½ cups chocolate-
   covered toffee
   chips

½ cup finely chopped
   blanched almonds

½ cup finely chopped
   milk chocolate

14 pop sticks

1. Line small baking sheet with plastic wrap. Scoop 14 rounded tablespoonfuls ice cream onto prepared baking sheet. Freeze 2 hours or until firm.

2. Combine toffee chips, almonds and chocolate in shallow dish; mix well.

3. Gently roll ice cream into balls in toffee mixture, turning to coat and pressing mixture evenly into ice cream. Return to baking sheet.*

4. Insert sticks. Freeze 2 hours or until firm.

If ice cream melts on baking sheet, place baking sheet and ice cream in freezer 30 minutes before continuing. If ice cream is too hard, let stand 1 to 2 minutes before rolling in toffee mixture.

Metric Conversion Chart

VOLUME MEASUREMENTS (dry)

⅛ teaspoon = 0.5 mL
¼ teaspoon = 1 mL
½ teaspoon = 2 mL
¾ teaspoon = 4 mL
1 teaspoon = 5 mL
1 tablespoon = 15 mL
2 tablespoons = 30 mL
¼ cup = 60 mL
⅓ cup = 75 mL
½ cup = 125 mL
⅔ cup = 150 mL
¾ cup = 175 mL
1 cup = 250 mL
2 cups = 1 pint = 500 mL
3 cups = 750 mL
4 cups = 1 quart = 1 L

VOLUME MEASUREMENTS (fluid)

1 fluid ounce (2 tablespoons) = 30 mL
4 fluid ounces (½ cup) = 125 mL
8 fluid ounces (1 cup) = 250 mL
12 fluid ounces (1½ cups) = 375 mL
16 fluid ounces (2 cups) = 500 mL

WEIGHTS (mass)

½ ounce = 15 g
1 ounce = 30 g
3 ounces = 90 g
4 ounces = 120 g
8 ounces = 225 g
10 ounces = 285 g
12 ounces = 360 g
16 ounces = 1 pound = 450 g

DIMENSIONS

1/16 inch = 2 mm
⅛ inch = 3 mm
¼ inch = 6 mm
½ inch = 1.5 cm
¾ inch = 2 cm
1 inch = 2.5 cm

OVEN TEMPERATURES

250°F = 120°C
275°F = 140°C
300°F = 150°C
325°F = 160°C
350°F = 180°C
375°F = 190°C
400°F = 200°C
425°F = 220°C
450°F = 230°C

BAKING PAN SIZES

Utensil	Size in Inches/Quarts	Metric Volume	Size in Centimeters
Baking or Cake Pan (square or rectangular)	8×8×2	2 L	20×20×5
	9×9×2	2.5 L	23×23×5
	12×8×2	3 L	30×20×5
	13×9×2	3.5 L	33×23×5
Loaf Pan	8×4×3	1.5 L	20×10×7
	9×5×3	2 L	23×13×7
Round Layer Cake Pan	8×1½	1.2 L	20×4
	9×1½	1.5 L	23×4
Pie Plate	8×1¼	750 mL	20×3
	9×1¼	1 L	23×3
Baking Dish or Casserole	1 quart	1 L	—
	1½ quart	1.5 L	—
	2 quart	2 L	—